The ABC's of the
IBM PC and Compatibles

The ABC's of the IBM® PC and Compatibles

Second Edition

Joan Lasselle
and
Carol Ramsay

SYBEX®

San Francisco · Paris · Düsseldorf · London

Book design by Thomas Ingalls + Associates
Cover photography by Casey Cartwright
Illustrations by Jeffrey James Giese

Dac-Easy is a trademark of Dac Software, Inc.
dBASE is a trademark of Ashton-Tate.
IBM PC, IBM PC/XT, IBM PC/AT, and PC-DOS are trademarks of International Business Machines
Corporation.
Lotus 1-2-3 is a trademark of Lotus Development Corporation.
Microsoft Windows and MS-DOS are trademarks of Microsoft Corporation.
PageMaker is a trademark of Aldus Corporation.
R:BASE is a trademark of Microrim, Inc.
Ventura Publisher is a trademark of Xerox Corporation.
WordPerfect is a trademark of WordPerfect Corporation.

First published under the title of *The ABC's of the IBM® PC*, Copyright 1984
ISBN: 0-89588-102-0

SYBEX is a registered trademark of SYBEX, Inc.

SYBEX is not affiliated with any manufacturer.

Library of Congress Card Number: 88-61536
ISBN 0-89588-370-8
Manufactured in the United States of America
10 9 8 7 6 5

Acknowledgments

We would like to thank our staff for making this new version of *The ABC's of the IBM PC* possible. Lisa Caras revised the original manuscript and tested this new edition for accuracy and usability. Brenda Keller proofread the manuscript and Kathy Seddiqui checked resources and provided a new user perspective.

We would also like to thank the SYBEX staff: Dianne King for getting a production slot, Joanne Cuthbertson for her editorial expertise, technical editors Joel Kroman and Daniel Tauber, technical illustrator Jeff Giese, pasteup artist Evelyn Ong-Sy, typesetters Aidan Wylde and Cheryl Vega, word processor Jocelyn B. Reynolds, proofreader Maria Mart, and indexer Julie Kawabata.

Contents at a Glance

Table of Contents

Introduction

Whether you have just purchased an IBM or IBM-compatible personal computer to use at home or whether you found one on your desk when you arrived at work this morning, this book is for you, the PC user.

We assume that you have little or no experience with PCs (or any other computer), and that you are not going to write your own programs—at least, not right away. Rather, you will be using purchased programs, called applications, such as Lotus 1-2-3 or Word-Perfect. You are anxious to learn the basics and put your PC to work. But where do you start?

This book is designed to get you started. Because you learn best by doing, we include exercises so that you can practice on your own PC as we go along. We will have you loading, entering, saving, and retrieving in no time. Here are the things we are going to talk about:

Chapter 1 introduces you to the parts of your PC: the hardware and the software. It describes the function of each component and discusses the different kinds of software applications you will probably be using.

Chapter 2 gets you started. You turn on the PC, load the operating system, set the date and time, and learn how to use the keyboard and diskette drive.

Chapter 3 shows you how to communicate with your PC using simple commands, menu selections, and function keys.

Chapter 4 tells you all about using diskettes. It includes proper handling, storage, labeling, and protection of diskettes. In addition, you will learn how to format and copy them.

Chapter 5 tells you how to organize the files on your hard disk. You learn how to create and use directories, how to name, list, copy, rename and delete files, and how to back up the important information in your system.

Chapter 6 discusses application programs in general.

Chapter 7 introduces you to WordPerfect and Lotus 1-2-3. Two short work sessions give you a feel for word processing and spreadsheets.

Chapter 8 describes additional components you can add to your PC to perform special functions, such as printing, graphics, and communications.

Chapter 9 gives you a checklist for problem-solving if things do not go as planned.

In addition, there are four appendices. One tells you how to unpack and set up your PC, another tells you how to perform all the exercises on a PC without a hard disk, and the final two give a glossary of terms and a list of resources.

What You Will Need

To use this book most successfully, you will need:

- An IBM or IBM-compatible PC so you can perform the operations as they are described;

- A copy of the DOS operating system (either PC-DOS or MS-DOS), which you might have to purchase separately from your computer dealer; and

- A little time. We have given you only the essentials—you will still need some time to try it all out.

This book uses an IBM PC/AT for examples that depend on a particular type of PC. If you have a different kind of IBM PC or a compatible PC from a computer manufacturer other than IBM, you may see slightly different messages or a key or control may be in a slightly different place. However, you should have no problem following the exercises.

We also assume you are using version 3.3 of DOS. If you are using another version, you should still be able to perform the exercises. The messages displayed on the screen may be different or a file we ask you to use may not be available. Use the examples we give you as models rather than performing them exactly.

If you want to sit down and use your PC for the first time, you are probably faced with one of two situations: the PC is cabled, connected, plugged in, and ready to go; or you are looking at a couple of large cardboard boxes and wondering where to start. If you need help putting your computer together, go to Appendix A where we tell you everything you need to know about setting up your PC.

Once that is done, you are ready for Chapter 1, which introduces you to the parts of your PC and talks about the different ways you can use it.

1

Anatomy of
Your PC

Featuring

*Basic hardware
components*

Software overview

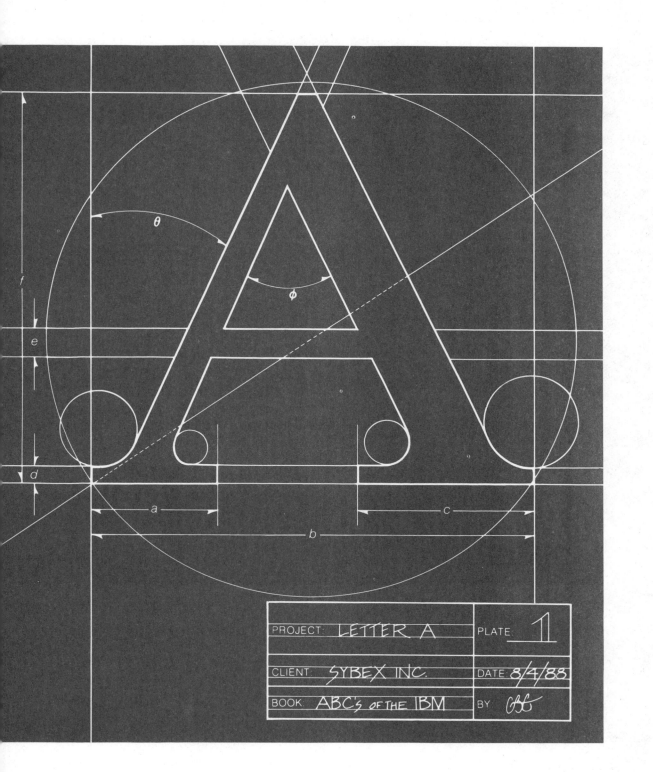

PROJECT: LETTER A   PLATE: 1

CLIENT: SYBEX INC.   DATE: 8/4/88

BOOK: ABC's OF THE IBM   BY: CBC

You probably already know that computers consist of both hardware and software. The *hardware* is the machine itself; the *software* is the information you use with it. A useful analogy is your stereo system; the stereo components are the equivalent of your computer's hardware, and the music (recorded on compact discs, tapes, and record albums) is the equivalent of software.

Let's begin by identifying the hardware components of your PC, as shown in Figure 1.1. Not all PCs have identical components, but most have the same basic components. In this chapter, we discuss those basic components. Refer to Chapter 8 for additional components that your PC may have.

*H*ardware

*T*he System Unit

The *system unit* is really the computer itself. It performs all operations, calculations, and processes; that is why it is often called the *central processing unit* or CPU. Inside are the electronic components, the microprocessor and printed-circuit boards that make the PC work.

The system unit contains the PC's *memory*. Memory is where your PC stores information and instructions as it processes them. Some information and instructions are stored permanently, and some are loaded into memory from a disk to be stored in memory temporarily. Temporary storage can be programs, such as the operating system or application software, or it can be the reports or information you use with the programs. Since your PC's memory capacity is limited, these programs and data are stored on your PC's hard disk when they are not being used, so that they do not take up valuable memory space.

*T*he Hard Disk Drive

The system unit also contains your PC's *hard disk drive*, also known as a *fixed disk drive*. The hard disk drive consists of a hard disk, a mechanism that spins the disk, a head that reads information from and writes information to the hard disk, and the electronics that

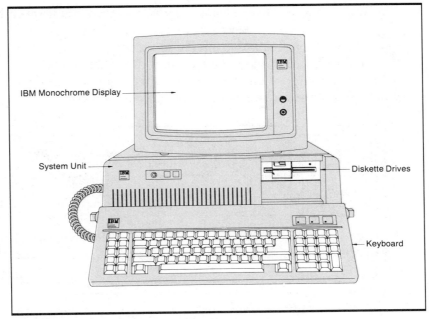
IBM Monochrome Display

System Unit

Diskette Drives

Keyboard

Figure 1.1: The IBM Personal Computer

make the disk drive work. The hard disk is sealed within the drive. As the hard disk spins within the drive, the head reads information from it and records information onto it.

Your hard disk stores the software you use with your PC. The hard disk contains the operating system programs that tell your PC how to work. As you work with your PC, you will also store application programs and information files on the hard disk.

*T*he Keyboard

You communicate with your PC by typing instructions and pressing keys on the *keyboard*. There are actually several types of PC keyboards. IBM produced three types: the original IBM PC and IBM PC/XT keyboard (see Figure 1.2), the IBM PC/AT keyboard (see Figure 1.3), and the enhanced keyboard for the PC/XT and PC/AT (see Figure 1.4). Although the layout of the keys are different on the three keyboards, each has all of the keys you will need to use. Find the one that best matches yours.

You will notice that the main part of the keyboard is much like a typewriter. The extra keys are used to perform special operations, sometimes alone and sometimes in conjunction with other keys.

If you can't find a key when we show it in a later illustration, refer back to the illustration of your keyboard on this page. From now on, we will assume you are using the enhanced keyboard.

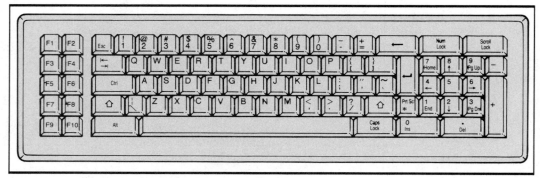

Figure 1.2: *The Original IBM PC Keyboard*

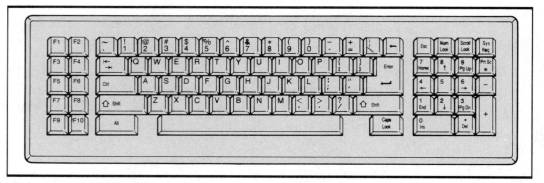

Figure 1.3: *The IBM PC/AT Keyboard*

If you are familiar with a typewriter or other keyboard, you know that one key sometimes serves two purposes. For example, you type 5 if you want a 5 but you hold down the Shift key and type 5 if you want a % sign. Many keys on the PC keyboard are used like the Shift key, giving different results when used with another key. You will learn about these keys throughout this book, especially in Chapter 3.

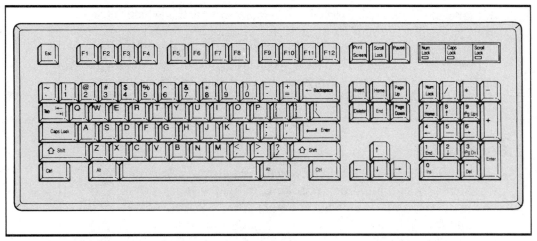

Figure 1.4: *The Enhanced Keyboard*

The keyboard itself is designed to be tilted or level, and is easily adjusted with the knobs on either side.

*T*he Diskette Drive

A *diskette drive* or *floppy disk drive* transfers information to and from your hard disk or directly into memory. Diskette drives read and record information on diskettes. Unlike your hard disk drive and hard disk, which are one unit, diskette drives and diskettes are separate; you can insert and remove diskettes from a diskette drive. You don't use diskettes to store information that you use often because diskette drives are slower and hold much less information than your hard disk. Instead, you can use diskettes to transfer information to and from your PC's hard disk. For example, software manufacturers distribute programs on diskette. You use such distribution diskettes to copy programs to your hard disk. Diskettes are also a good way to transfer information from your PC to another or to store copies of the information on your hard disk.

This book assumes that you have a hard disk and one diskette drive. The diskette drive is called A:, and the hard disk is called C:. They are not labeled, so you will just have to remember which is which. However, you will use them so often that remembering won't be much of a problem.

If your PC does not have a hard disk drive, you can store all of your information on diskettes. Appendix B gives you additional instructions for using a PC with no hard disk.

The Display

Different people call the display by different names. You might hear it referred to as a monitor, console, CRT (cathode ray tube), VDU (video display unit), terminal, or, simply, screen. Whatever you call it, its function is to display what you type on the keyboard, give you instructions, ask you questions, and present you with information.

Your computer does not need a display to do its job, but *you* need it so that you have an idea of what is going on. Without a display, you do not know what you are typing and your PC has no way to communicate with you. A display is really more of a necessity than an option, although it is often purchased separately. In addition to the display, you need an adapter that plugs into your PC.

For simplicity, we assume that you have an IBM Monochrome Display, but you can use other displays, including a regular home TV set. If you want to use the PC with your TV set, you will have to buy a special adapter, called an RF modulator, to convert the signal that the PC puts out into one that the TV can understand. Consult your PC operations guide for more information.

The knobs on the front of the IBM display are used to adjust the contrast and brightness of the screen, just like a TV. On your display, the controls may not be on the front.

The Mouse

Your PC may also have a *mouse*, like the one shown in Figure 1.5. Your PC's mouse is not an animal, but a small device that sits to the side of your keyboard. Some programs use the mouse to control a pointer on the display. You move the pointer by moving the mouse on your desk. If you move the mouse to the right, the pointer moves to the right; if you move the mouse to the left, the pointer moves to the left; and so on. You might use the pointer to draw and move shapes in a graphics program, or to select text and commands in a word processing program.

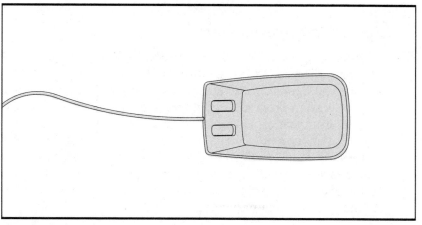

Figure 1.5: A Mouse

Software

You will be using three kinds of software with your PC: the disk operating system, application programs, and the information and reports you create with the application programs. A fourth kind, called an operating environment, is optional. You store software on your hard disk and on diskettes.

The Disk Operating System

The *disk operating system* coordinates the interaction between the hardware and software, most importantly the transfer of information between the memory in the system unit and the disk drives (which are sometimes called external memory). It also coordinates other activities such as printing.

Your PC uses an operating system called DOS (or more formally PC-DOS or MS-DOS, depending on who sold it to you). Even though

you cannot operate your computer without DOS, you normally do
not automatically receive a copy of it when you purchase your PC.
You have to buy it separately.

*O*perating Environments

Operating environments are programs that change the way you
interact with your PC. The most popular is Microsoft Windows. Normally, you interact with your PC by typing DOS commands, loading
an application program, and working with one file at a time. Operating environment programs let you work with several applications and
files at the same time. Usually, they display files in *windows* on your
screen. Windows, shown in Figure 1.6, are like sheets of paper; you
can move them, change their size, and stack them on top of each
other. Instead of typing commands, you use a mouse to select commands from menus and manipulate the windows on your screen.

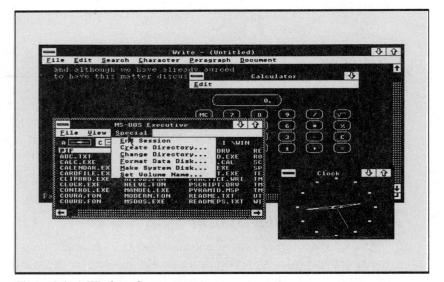

Figure 1.6: A Windows Screen

If you have a program such as Microsoft Windows on your PC,
you can use a DOS window to follow the examples in this book and
learn about DOS. Read the documentation that came with the program to learn how to display a DOS window.

*A*pplication Programs

Application programs operate in conjunction with DOS so that you can perform useful tasks with your PC without having to be a programmer. There are thousands of application programs available that convert your PC into a tool to increase productivity and decrease paperwork. The most popular programs can be grouped into six categories: word processors, spreadsheets, database management programs, payroll and accounting programs, graphics, and desktop publishing. A seventh category, games, converts your PC into an entertainment center.

Chances are, if you are using your PC at home or in the office, you will be using one or more of these kinds of programs. So let's take a look at what each of them can do for you.

Word Processors

Word processors turn your PC into a super typewriter. Currently, the most popular word processing program is WordPerfect—we introduce you to it in Chapter 7.

With a word processor you compose text using your PC keyboard just as you would use a typewriter keyboard. However, because the characters are recorded electronically rather than on paper, you can correct your mistakes and make any changes you want before printing the text out on a printer. You can erase words, phrases, or whole blocks of text, insert new ones, or move them from one place to another with a few keystrokes. Then you can store your document on a diskette and go back to it at any time. You can print it or revise it whenever you want, or you can copy it and store multiple versions of the same document.

One of the real benefits of word-processing programs is that you can view your document on your PC's display before printing it out. If you don't like what you see, you can change margins, line spacing, or tab settings and see the effect immediately on the screen. This is called *on-screen formatting*. You see only the portion of the document that can fit on your screen at one time, but that does not mean that the size of your document is limited to the size of your screen. You can move backwards and forwards through the document as you wish, looking at a page or section at a time. This is called *paging* or *scrolling*.

In some offices, a few PCs may be used only for word processing. These dedicated machines are probably in the hands of secretaries who can really make them produce. However, because of word processing, typing is no longer just for secretaries. Many office professionals use word processors to compose reports or letters and to jot off memos or notes. In addition, a large group of professional writers feel that their wildest dreams have come true!

Spreadsheets

We talk about spreadsheets in more detail in Chapter 7, so we will just give you a brief introduction here.

All electronic spreadsheets are based on the same idea. You are given an electronic worksheet or grid made up of rows and columns. The intersection of each row and column is called a cell. You can set up a typical financial report or model by entering column and row labels such as Sales, Expenses, or Profit and the appropriate data—either numbers or formulas. The numbers represent variables and the formulas maintain their relationship between the variables. If the values (numbers) change, all related values change. If you change a variable value, all related values change on the basis of the formula. If you change the relationship by changing the formula, again, all affected entries are changed.

Spreadsheets make it easy to play the *What If?* game. Once your model is established, you can use it to see the potential effect of different decisions. What if expenses increase? What if sales decrease? What about expanding? Where is the breakeven point? At home, you can analyze stock purchase decisions, figure your income tax, or decide whether it is more cost effective to rent or buy that piece of equipment.

Lotus 1-2-3 is currently the most popular PC spreadsheet. However, its popularity has spawned lots of similar products, many of which you can use with your PC.

Database Management Programs

Databases are large pools of information, which can be numbers or text. You can use a database management program to search for a particular piece of information, to find all information in the database fitting certain criteria, or to sort the information in specified ways. Databases can be used with other programs such as word processors or spreadsheets.

Databases can be extremely large, such as one an airline uses for issuing passengers' tickets, or very small, such as one that keeps a list of the employees in your department.

Two popular database programs are dBASE and R:BASE. Both programs allow you to collect and categorize information, and then retrieve it in different forms. However, they each do some things better than others, so you need to pick the product best suited to your project.

Payroll and Accounting Programs

If you run a small business, you can use an accounting application for your payroll, accounts payable and receivable, and general ledger. If you have the kind of business where everyone wears lots of hats, computerized accounting can free up time to focus on the business of the business rather than the bookkeeping.

In the past, many small businesses have bought accounting services from a bank or computer service center. With a PC, you can buy an application program (for example, Dac-Easy) and do your own accounting, probably for less money.

Graphics

Graphics programs let you display information as a graph or chart. You can display pie charts, bar and line graphs, or scatter-grams. Graphics programs make it easy to summarize large amounts of data or to identify trends. Often graphs are used in reports or as presentation aids.

Graphics programs are very useful; however, they require special hardware. For example, you must add a special graphics board to your system unit as well as a graphics monitor (usually a color monitor). In addition, you may need to buy a special printer or plotter so that you can make a copy on paper of the graph or chart that is displayed on your screen.

Desktop Publishing

Desktop publishing programs let you produce documents that look like they came off a printing press. You can combine different styles and sizes of text with graphics on the same page. Such programs use a graphics display to show your document. What you see on your screen is exactly what you get when you print your document with a high-quality printer. You don't have to be a magazine or newspaper publisher to benefit from using a desktop publishing program. With desktop publishing, you can produce impressive-looking reports, proposals, and newsletters.

Two popular desktop publishing programs are Ventura Publisher and PageMaker. Each operates differently. If you plan to do desktop publishing, you should take a look at the type of documents you will produce and determine what capabilities you require before you choose a program.

Games

At home, games are a popular use for the PC. Like everything else, some are good and some are bad—the choice is pretty broad. Some of the best games include animation and lively graphics as well as different levels of expertise.

While games do not generally help get the job done at the office, they are good forms of relaxation and some people feel they sharpen problem-solving skills and hand-eye coordination.

Now that you know what you will be working with in terms of both hardware and software, you are ready to begin using your PC.

*R*eview

Your computer has the following hardware components:

- The system unit
- The hard disk
- The keyboard

- The diskette drives
- The display

There are four kinds of PC software:

- Disk operating systems
- Operating environments
- Application programs
- The reports and information you use with your application programs

There are seven common types of application programs:

- Word processors
- Spreadsheets
- Database management programs
- Payroll and accounting programs
- Graphics
- Desktop publishing programs
- Games

2

Beginning with the Basics

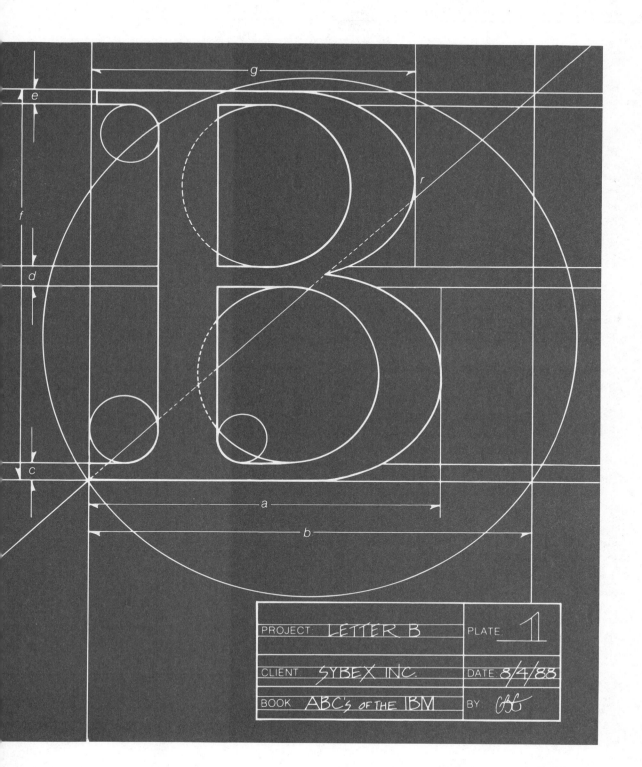

PROJECT: LETTER B   PLATE: 1

CLIENT: SYBEX INC.   DATE: 8/4/88

BOOK: ABC's of the IBM   BY:

Now that you are familiar with the parts of your PC and have an idea of some of the things you can do with it, you are ready to start using your PC for the first time. But before you go any further, check two things:

- Is your PC plugged in?
- Has DOS been installed on your hard disk? Most computer dealers will install it for you when you purchase your PC.

Yes to both questions? If DOS has not been installed, find someone to do it for you. Although your DOS reference manual gives you instructions for preparing your hard disk and installing DOS on it, this can be a complicated process. It is better to have an expert do it for you.

Turning On Your PC

Turning on your PC is just a matter of following these steps:

1. Turn the knobs on the front of the display fully to the right (your monitor may not have these controls in the front). These are the contrast and brightness knobs. Once your PC is warmed up, you can adjust them, but if you don't start with them fully on, you might not see anything on the screen.

2. Turn on the power with the switch on the right side of the system unit (some PCs have the power switch on the back).

Your PC runs through a quick test to make sure everything is in working order. If the test is successful, you hear a short beep. Next you see information about the version of DOS that your computer is loading.

Setting the Date and Time

When you load DOS, your PC asks you for the current date and time by displaying the following message:

Current date is Thu 1-01-1980
Enter new date:_

If your PC enters the date and time automatically, you won't see this message. Instead your PC will load DOS and immediately display the DOS prompt, which is described later in this chapter. Read the instructions for setting the date and time anyway. They show you how to enter information into your PC.

You do not have to set the date and time, but doing so now can prove useful later on. Then, when you store information in a file, DOS automatically stores the precise date and time with the file. Should you have more than one version of the same file, you can check the date later to see which version is most current. If you have not set the date, the existing date will be used as the date for every file.

The most common way to enter the date is month/day/year, as in 4/12/89, though 4-12-89 is also acceptable. You can use several formats for the date and time, but some are not acceptable. For example, July 4th will not work since DOS accepts only numbers in the date. Time is usually entered as hours:minutes or hours:minutes:seconds, as in 10:05 or 15:45:24. You can also add hundredths of seconds. Refer to your DOS reference manual for a list of all the acceptable formats.

If you use a format that is not acceptable, DOS flashes Invalid Date or Invalid time on the screen and lets you try again.

Your PC is waiting for you to enter a new date so go ahead and type in today's date immediately after Enter new date:. For example,

Enter new date:5-25-89

*T*he Cursor

The blinking underscore you see after date: is called the *cursor.* It marks the position on the screen where the next character you type will appear. You will see the cursor move about as you enter and change information. In a moment, we will tell you how to make the cursor move wherever you want it to (see the section "The Numeric Keypad and the Arrow Keys").

*C*orrecting Mistakes

If you make a mistake, press the Backspace key (←) to go back to the point of the error and retype correctly (see Figure 2.1). Notice that each time you press ←, the character to the left of the cursor is erased and the cursor moves back one space. In this way, you can backspace over an error to erase it, then retype the correct characters. If you are a perfect typist, you might want to make some deliberate mistakes so that you can practice erasing them.

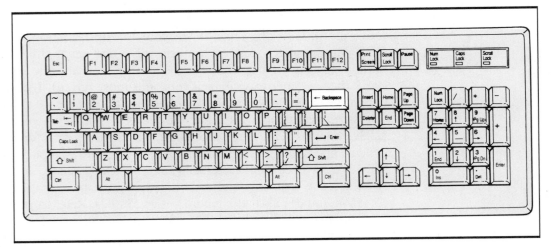

Figure 2.1: *The Backspace Key*

*E*ntering What You Have Typed

The Enter key (⏎) on your PC keyboard replaces the Return key on a typewriter keyboard (see Figure 2.2). Sometimes you will use it like the Return key, but usually you will use it to enter an instruction into the computer. Although the information you type on the keyboard is displayed on the screen, the computer has no knowledge of it until you enter it by pressing ⏎ to finalize the operation.

1. When you are satisfied that your typing is flawless, enter the date by pressing ⏎.

2. If you do not want to set the date, just press ⏎ without typing anything.

3. Your PC displays the current-time message. For example,

Current time is: 0:01:47:94
Enter new time:_

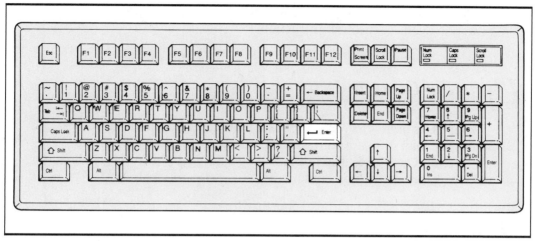

Figure 2.2: *The Enter Key (◄─┘)*

4. Type the time after Enter new time:. For example,

   Enter new time: 15:30:00

5. If you typed the time correctly, press ◄─┘ to enter it.

6. If you do not want to set the time, just press ◄─┘ without typing anything.

7. At this point the DOS copyright statement and prompt appear on the screen. They look like this:

   The IBM Personal Computer DOS
   Version 3.30 (C) Copyright International Business Machines
   Corp 1981, 1987
   (C) Copyright Microsoft Corp 1981, 1987

   C>

The DOS Prompt

Once DOS is loaded and the date and time are set, your screen displays C>. This is the *DOS prompt*, sometimes called the C prompt, and it tells you that DOS has been loaded successfully.

The C tells you that DOS is using drive C: as the current drive—unless you tell it otherwise, it will always expect to find the information it needs on your hard disk—drive C:. The > symbol says *OK, I'm ready. Tell me what to do next.* That is why it is called a *prompt;* it is prompting you for the next instruction.

Using the Diskette Drive

Your PC is useless to you without software to make it do what you want. You load software onto your PC's hard disk by copying it from a diskette. Therefore, it is important to know how to insert and remove diskettes. Let's practice.

Inserting a Diskette

1. Find your DOS operating diskette. This is one of the diskettes your dealer used to install DOS on your hard disk. In case you accidentally lose the information on your hard disk, you can use this diskette to reinstall DOS. You should find this diskette in a plastic holder in the back of your DOS reference manual.

2. Hold the diskette with the label up, right thumb on the label, and slide it out of its paper sleeve. Be careful not to touch the surfaces that are exposed through the cutouts on the diskette jacket. (If you are lost already, take a look at Figure 2.3.)

3. Open the door of your diskette drive if it is not already open.

4. Push the diskette gently into the drive, being careful not to bend it. Make sure it is fully inserted.

5. Close the drive door.

Changing the Current Drive

Remember that DOS is installed on your hard disk, drive C:. When you turn on your PC, drive C: is the current drive. You might decide to put a diskette in your diskette drive, drive A:, and start working with it instead. In that case, there would be no point in keeping drive C: as the current drive.

To move to drive A:, you are going to have to type A:. Use the shift key to type a colon (:) just as you would on a typewriter.

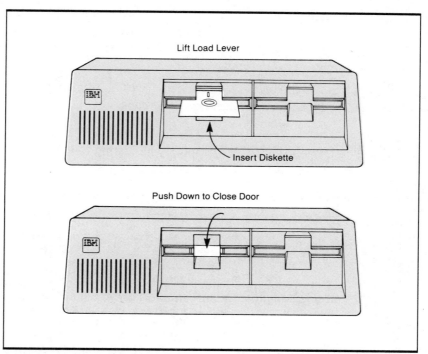

Figure 2.3: *Inserting a Diskette*

*T*he Shift Keys

The ⇧ keys on your PC keyboard replace the Shift keys on a typewriter keyboard (see Figure 2.4). As with a typewriter, you can use them to type capital letters, symbols such as %, and some punctuation marks, including :.

Now practice moving from one drive to another.

1. The last line on your screen reads

    C>_

    You move to drive A: by typing A: ↵ immediately after C>. The last line now reads

    C>A:

This changes the DOS prompt to A> and tells DOS to look at the diskette in drive A: for further instructions. This is sometimes called logging onto drive A: and Drive A: then becomes the *logged* or *default* drive.

2. When you are ready to go back to drive C:, immediately after A> type C: ←⎯. The last line now reads

   A>C:

   The DOS prompt C> reappears, indicating that drive C: is the current (or logged) drive once again.

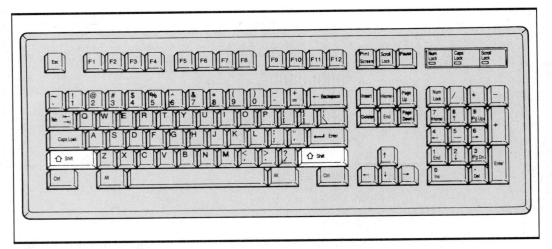

Figure 2.4: The Shift Keys

*R*emoving a Diskette

Now, remove the diskette.

1. Open the drive door.

2. Remove the diskette without bending it or touching the exposed surfaces.

3. Replace the diskette in its paper sleeve.

Keep the DOS diskette nearby. You will use it in the next chapter when we show you commands for your PC.

Getting Familiar with the Keyboard

As you have realized by now, you communicate with your IBM PC by typing on the keyboard. You can enter commands and information, respond to prompts, and select different options or functions. All your word-processing and spreadsheet reports will be entered from the keyboard, as well as any information you want to use with other application programs.

Your PC keyboard is arranged similarly to a typewriter keyboard. Most of the keys are marked just as they are on a typewriter with a few notable exceptions. You already know about the Enter key (←—┘), the Backspace key (←—), and the Shift key (⇧). The Tab key, which works like a typewriter Tab key, is marked ⇆. But what are all those other keys?

There are three additional sets of keys on the PC keyboard that you will not find on a typewriter keyboard: the numeric keypad, including the cursor-positioning (arrow) keys; the function keys; and several control keys, the most important of which, for right now, are the Ctrl and Esc keys.

The Numeric Keypad and the Arrow Keys

When you press the key marked Num Lock (see Figure 2.5), you can use the numeric keypad located on the right of your keyboard to enter numbers. If you are going to use application programs that require lots of numbers, the numeric pad can be very handy, especially if you already know how to operate a ten-key calculator by touch.

When the Num Lock key is off (simply press it again to turn it off), you can use the keys marked with an arrow to position the cursor. The arrow keys move the cursor up, down, to the right, and to the left. You can also use the keys marked Home, PgUp, PgDown, and End to move the cursor. These keys can have a special meaning for different application programs you may be using. Be sure to consult the reference manual for that program to find out what they mean.

When Num Lock is on, you can't use the arrow or other cursor movement keys. For that reason, IBM has provided a duplicate set of

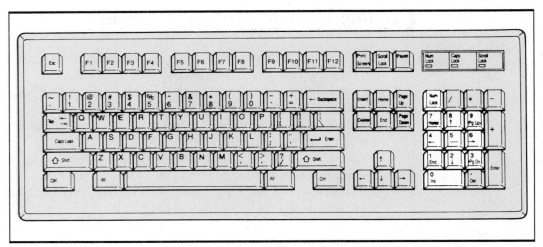

Figure 2.5: *The Numeric Keypad, the Arrow Keys, and the Num Lock Key*

cursor keys on the enhanced keyboard (located between the standard
keyboard and the numeric keypad). You may find it more convenient
to use these cursor movement keys all of the time, even when Num
Lock is off.

The Function Keys

Figure 2.6 shows the twelve function keys (F1 to F12) positioned at
the top of your keyboard. If you have an older keyboard, your ten
function keys will be grouped together on the left. These keys perform
predefined tasks that change from application to application. We will
tell you more about them when we show you how to tell your PC what
to do.

The Ctrl Key

Remember that we said in Chapter 1 that some keys are used with
other keys to add another dimension to your keyboard? For example,
the key marked j becomes J when used with the Shift key. The Ctrl key
(see Figure 2.7) works the same way.

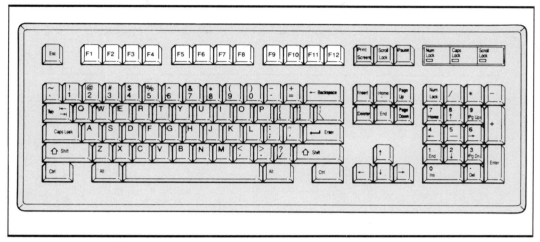

Figure 2.6: *The Function Keys*

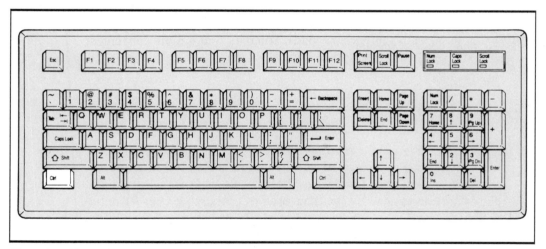

Figure 2.7: *The Ctrl Key*

The Esc Key

The Esc (escape) key (see Figure 2.8) may perform different functions in different application programs, but basically it is used to get you out of situations you don't want to be in. It is also used to interrupt programs or commands. Some programs will ask you to confirm that you really want to interrupt the process; others will assume that you know what you are doing. Check the program documentation to find out exactly how the Esc key works for that program.

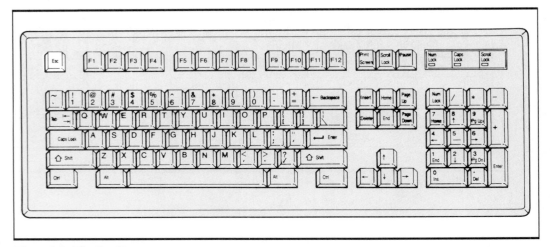

Figure 2.8: The Esc Key

*R*esetting Your PC

Your PC does not do anything without *your* instructions. However, you might accidentally type a wrong command or press a wrong key and lose control of what it is doing. There's no need to panic, you can always regain control by resetting your PC. Resetting your PC interrupts whatever it is doing and reloads DOS. If you reset from within an application, you may lose the information that you created since you last saved your file. If you save often, losing information is a small sacrifice compared to knowing that you are truly in control.

1. As shown in Figure 2.9, hold down the Ctrl and Alt keys on the left of the keyboard, and press the Del key on the right. (Sound like a lot of keys to press at once? It is. You don't want to accidentally reset your PC.)

2. Your PC loads DOS from the hard disk. When it finishes you
   see the current-date message. For example,

   Current date is Tue 1-01-1980
   Enter new date:_

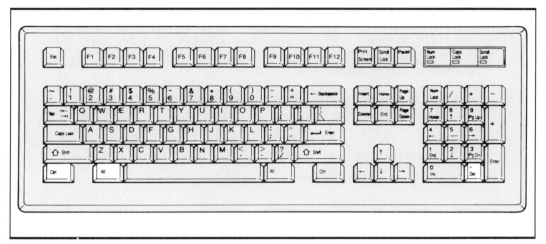

Figure 2.9: The Ctrl, Alt, and Del Keys

*T*urning off Your PC

You turn off your PC by turning off the power switch. If you turn
off your PC while the hard disk drive is in the process of reading or
writing information on the hard disk, you could accidentally damage
your hard disk. To prevent such damage, most PCs automatically shut
down the hard disk before they turn off. Others give you a special
command, called Shutdown or Park, for shutting down your hard
disk before you turn off your PC. Check your operations manual for
instructions on properly turning off your PC.

So that starts you out. You always turn on the machine, load DOS,
and optionally set the date and time to begin. These steps will become
second nature soon, but until they do, here is a quick review of the
points in this chapter.

Review

To turn on the computer:

- Be sure the power cord is connected to the system unit and plugged into a live outlet.
- Turn on the power switch on the right side of the system unit.

To adjust the keyboard and screen brightness:

- Use the knobs on the side of the keyboard to tilt or lower the keyboard.
- Use the knobs on the front of the display screen to adjust the brightness and contrast.

The date and time:

- Can be reset every time you turn on your PC.
- Can be saved with any files you store on disk.
- Allows you to check for the most current information.

To correct mistakes:

- Use the Backspace key (⟵).

To enter what you have typed:

- Use the Enter key (⟵⟂).

To insert a diskette in the diskette drive:

- Hold the diskette with the label up, right thumb on the label, and slide it out of its paper sleeve.
- Open the diskette drive door.
- Push the diskette gently into the drive.
- Close the drive door.

To change the current drive:

- Type the drive identifier (A or C) followed by a : (for example, C:).

Additional keys:

- The numeric keypad, including the cursor-positioning (arrow) keys
- The duplicate cursor movement keys
- The function keys
- The Ctrl key
- The Esc key

To reset your PC:

- Hold down the Ctrl and Alt keys, and press the Del key.

To turn off your PC:

- Check whether or not you need to shut down your hard disk separately.
- Turn off the power switch.

3

Commands
for Your PC

Featuring

Typing commands
Canceling commands
Using menus
Using function keys

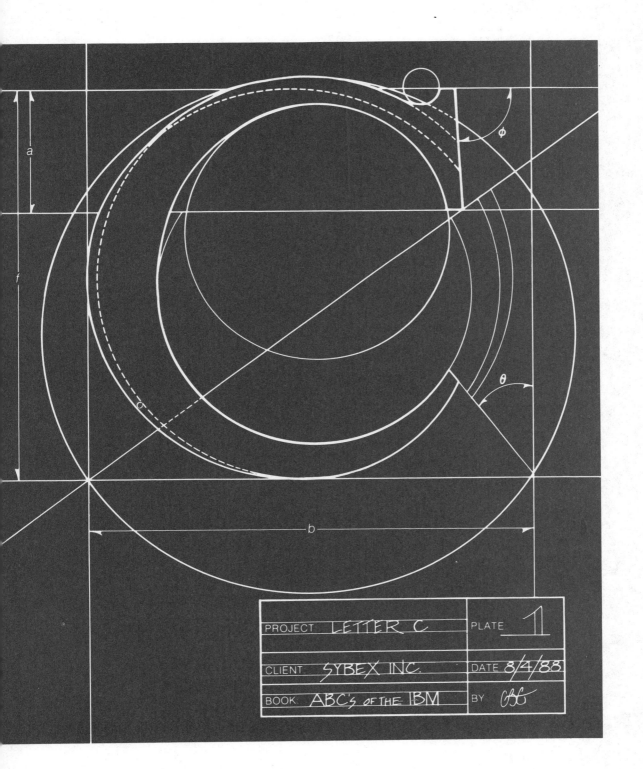

a

f

φ

θ

σ

b

PROJECT LETTER C   PLATE 1

CLIENT SYBEX INC.   DATE 8/4/88

BOOK ABC's of the IBM   BY CBG

Your PC is a willing servant provided you tell it exactly what you want it to do. Today's reality doesn't let you speak to your PC; however, you can communicate easily and effectively by using commands.

Commands are typed, selected from a list of command options, or chosen by pressing the function key associated with the command. The method depends on the software that you are using. For example, DOS, your computer's operating system, responds to commands that you type.

Typing Commands

Typed commands are words that have special meanings. With them, you instruct your PC to perform specific tasks. Each software application has its own set of commands. However, once you become familiar with different applications, you will see that they have some commands in common.

The typed commands you use with your PC are related to the task you want the software to perform. Sometimes the command name directly reflects the task. For example, LIST, PRINT, and DELETE are common commands that are used with many software applications. However, most of the time the command is expressed in a kind of shorthand. The command DIR, for example, lists all the files in the directory and the command CHKDSK checks the amount of space available on the diskette. Occasionally the commands are not that easy to figure out—GRAFTABL, for example. (Don't worry about what that means for now.)

When you give instructions to people, you often have to give some extra information so that they know exactly what to do. For example, if you give the command *Go*, do you mean *Go to the store* or *Go to the movies?* Software commands are the same. You often have to give additional information so the computer will do exactly what you want.

The extra information you give when you enter a command is called a *parameter*. Each command has its own set of parameters for which you must supply specific values. For example, if you give your computer the command COPY, your computer needs to know *what* you want it to copy. The name of the file you want copied is a parameter of the command, and you would have to supply the file name in order for the command to be carried out.

Another thing about commands—you must enter them exactly as they are shown in the software's reference manual or the computer will not know what you mean. Type a command incorrectly and your PC will be stumped! It will flash a message like Bad command name or File not found at you and you will have to enter the command again.

That goes for parameters, too—you need to enter them in a precise way. Type them correctly, and enter them in the correct order. If you change the order, the computer will not know how to interpret the command, or will do something that you did not intend it to do.

We're going to try giving commands using the DOS command DIR as an example. The DIR command tells DOS to display a list of all the files stored on a disk or in a directory. DOS gives you the file name, the type of file, the size, and the date and time created. For example,

APPEND	EXE	5825	3-17-87	12:00p
ASSIGN	COM	1561	3-17-87	12:00p
ATTRIB	EXE	9529	3-17-87	12:00p
.	.	.	.	.
.	.	.	.	.
BASICA	PIF	2048	3-17-87	12:00p
MORTGAGE	BAS	6251	3-17-87	12:00p
32 File(s)	9216 bytes free			

It also tells you the total number of files on the disk; in this case, 32.

Want to give it a try? Because you may not have many files on your hard disk yet, let's list the files on the DOS operating diskette. Follow these steps:

1. If it is not already on, turn on your PC now. Enter the date and time (if your PC does not do so automatically). When DOS has loaded, you see the C> prompt.

2. Insert your DOS diskette into the diskette drive.

3. Change the current drive to the diskette drive. Immediately after the DOS prompt C>, type

   A: ↵

4. Immediately after the A> prompt, type

   DIR ↩

   and watch what happens. Did the information move up off the screen faster than you could read it? When this happens, you will want to *freeze*, or stop, the display.

Freezing the Display

The display screen on your PC is really a window that shows only a portion of the information available to you. As you fill the screen with information it moves up, one line at a time, out of your view. This is called *scrolling*.

You can stop the display from scrolling out of view by using the Ctrl key with the Num Lock key (see Figure 3.1). Let's try it.

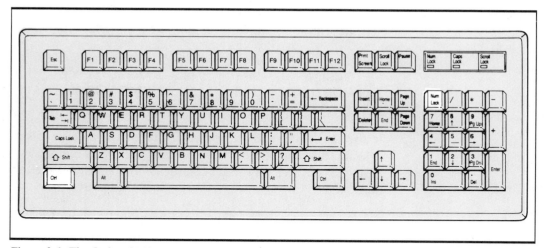

Figure 3.1: The Ctrl and Num Lock Keys

1. Type:

   DIR ↩

2. As soon as the display starts to scroll up, hold down the Ctrl key and press the Num Lock key to freeze the display on the screen. Too fast? Go back to step 1 and try again. (You can also hold down the Ctrl key and press S. Is this easier for you?)

3. When you are ready to start the display scrolling again, simply press any key. Now let's try using the DIR command with a parameter (that extra information you can use with commands).

4. You can use a file name as a parameter to display information about one particular file. For example, when you type

DIR COMMAND ⟵

your PC displays the following on your screen:

COMMAND　COM　25307　3-17-87　12:00p
1 File(s)　10000 bytes free

If your version of DOS is different from ours, you may see a different date.

Upper- and Lowercase

With DOS (and many other operating systems), it does not matter whether you enter commands in uppercase (capital) letters or lowercase letters.

1. Type the DIR command again, sometimes using the Shift key for uppercase letters and sometimes not; for example,

Dir ⟵
DIR ⟵
dir ⟵

You will see that the result is the same whether you enter the commands in lowercase or uppercase or a mixture of the two.

The Caps Lock Key

If you want to type in all capitals, you can use the Caps Lock key instead of having to hold down the ⇧ key. The Caps Lock key works only with the letters on your keyboard. You will still be able to type ; or / and you will still have to use the ⇧ key to type a % symbol.

The Caps Lock key is like an on/off key—press it once to type all capitals, and press it again to stop typing capitals. On some keyboards, the key does not stay down and there is nothing to indicate that you have pressed it, so you just have to remember. Whether you are using DOS commands or other software on your PC, the Caps Lock key works the same way.

Now enter some commands using the Caps Lock key.

1. Press the Caps Lock key and type:

   DIR ←
   DIR COMMAND ←

   These commands give the same results as before.

2. When you have finished typing all capitals, press the Caps Lock key again to turn it off.

*C*anceling a Command

Suppose you typed DIR COMMEND instead of DIR COM-MAND. How would you cancel the command so that you could enter it correctly?

You can cancel a command before you press ← by holding down the Ctrl key and pressing the Break key (located on either the Scroll Lock key or the Pause Key, depending on your keyboard; see Figure 3.2). The Break key cancels the command completely so long as you have not pressed ←. The computer will display ^C to tell you the command has been cancelled. You can then go on with whatever you meant to do.

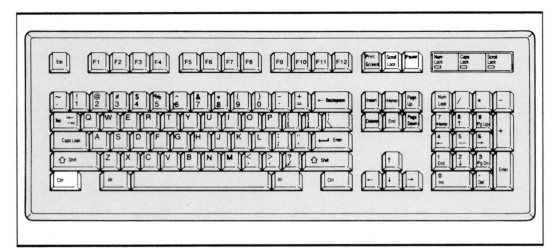

Figure 3.2: *The Ctrl and Break Keys*

Use the DIR command again to see how canceling a command works.

1. Type

   DIR (Do not press ◄─┘)

2. To cancel the command, hold down the Ctrl key and press the Break key.

That's enough about typed commands for now. Let's look at another way of telling your PC what to do.

Choosing From Menus

Some software lets you perform functions by selecting them from several options displayed on a list called a *command menu*. A command menu is like a menu in a restaurant. It lists your choices and you select the one you want.

Software menus usually list the options with letters or numbers in front of them. You make your selection by typing the letter or number. Sometimes you select an option by typing the first letter of its name. If your PC has a mouse, you can use it to point at a menu choice and then press a button on the mouse to select that choice. Figure 3.3 shows a sample menu.

Using the menu in Figure 3.3, you would type A to load a file, B to name a file, and so on.

Software designers use menus rather than typed commands because they make the software easier to use. First of all, they eliminate lots of

```
A- LOAD FILE
B- SAVE FILE
C- RENAME FILE
D - PRINT FILE
```

Figure 3.3: A Sample Menu

typing. The command or a description of a function is listed on the menu and you only have to type the letter or number that refers to the one you want. This helps people who are not used to using keyboards communicate with their computer.

The second reason designers use menus is that they make it easier for you to decide what you want by giving you a frame of reference. Also, you do not have to remember a lot of command formats because the menu reminds you how to give an instruction to your computer.

Want to try your hand with menus? We show you how to use menus in Chapter 7 with the spreadsheet program Lotus 1-2-3.

Using the Function Keys

Another way you can communicate with your computer is through function keys. As you know, the function keys are the row of keys at the top of the keyboard labeled F1 through F12. (On some keyboards the function keys are two rows of keys on the left of the keyboard.) You use these function keys with many software applications, so take a minute to get used to their layout.

When a software application program uses the function keys, it pre-defines each one of the keys to perform a specific operation. The function each key performs changes from application to application and can even change within a program.

At this point you are probably wondering *But how do I know which key does what when?* A very good question. Most programs that use function keys save you a lot of confusion by displaying the current meaning of the function keys on the screen, so you can tell which key to use. Others give you a template to place around the function keys on your keyboard. The template reminds you of each key's function.

We give you examples of how to use function keys when we introduce you to WordPerfect in Chapter 7.

*R*eview

Three ways to tell your PC what to do:

- Type a command (a precise word or group of words).
- Choose a menu option by typing its letter or number. (If you have a mouse, point to the menu option and press a mouse button. Refer to your software documentation for instructions.)
- Choose one of the function keys (F1 through F12 on the keyboard) that corresponds to a screen label.

Use the DIR command to:

- List all files on the diskette.
- List a single file when you include the file name with the command.

To stop the display from scrolling out of view:

- Hold down Ctrl and press Num Lock (or Ctrl and S) to freeze the display.
- Press any key to start it again.

To type in capitals:

- The Shift Key (⇧) gives an uppercase letter or a symbol from the top row.
- The Caps Lock key gives all capitals; press it once for all capitals, press it again to end capitals.

To cancel a command:

- Hold down Ctrl and press Break.

4

All About
Diskettes

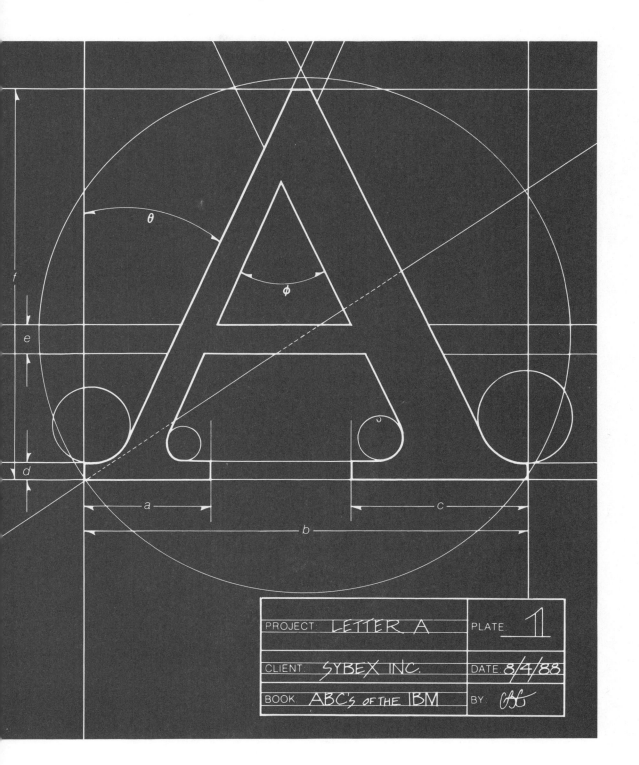

PROJECT: LETTER A   PLATE: 1

CLIENT: SYBEX INC.   DATE: 8/4/88

BOOK: ABC's of the IBM   BY: CBC

Without information that tells it how to work, your PC is useless. Normally, you keep the information that your PC needs on its hard disk. But how do you get it there in the first place? DOS and almost all applications are distributed on diskettes. You will often use diskettes to copy new information onto your hard disk and store copies of important information from your hard disk.

Diskettes are also known as *floppy disks* or *floppies*. They are called floppy because they bend easily. For this reason they have a protective covering that keeps them flat. The actual diskette on which information is stored spins inside this cover. Information is read from and written to the PC's memory by a read-write head (similar to the playing arm on a record player) from the cut out area on the diskette.

Diskettes come in three sizes: 8-inch, 5¼-inch, and 3½-inch. The diskettes you use match the size of your diskette drives. The oldest diskettes are 8-inch; PC's do not use them. Most PCs use 5¼-inch diskettes; however, some newer PCs use 3½-inch diskettes.

It is not important that you understand how information is stored on a diskette; however, a couple of points can help you out on your first trip to your computer store. The type of diskette you choose must be compatible with your diskette drive.

First, information can be stored on one or both sides of a diskette. Diskettes that use only one side are called *single-sided* and those that use both sides are called *double-sided*. Most PC's use double-sided diskettes; however, your diskette drive may be single-sided.

Second, the way information is stored on a diskette can vary. Some 5 ¼-inch diskettes (see Figure 4.1) are *single-density*, some are *double-density*, and others are *high-density*. Density simply refers to how the diskette stores characters as magnetic impulses. A double-density diskette can store twice as many characters (360 kilobytes) in the same amount of space as a single-density diskette. A high-density diskette can store four times as many characters (1.2 megabytes) as a double-density diskette.

In this chapter, we will talk about how to handle, label, store, and copy your diskettes, but first of all, here are a few general rules to follow. These are the DON'Ts. They are here at the beginning so they are sure to catch your attention.

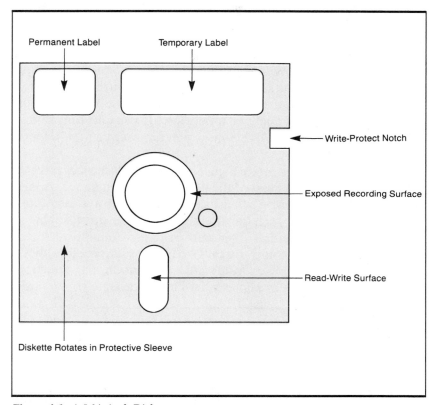

Figure 4.1: *A 5 ¹/₄-inch Diskette*

Rules for Handling Diskettes

- DON'T touch the exposed surfaces of a diskette.
- DON'T bend or fold a diskette.
- DON'T write on diskette labels with a sharp pencil or ball point pen.
- DON'T put diskettes near magnetized objects.
- DON'T put them in places that are very hot or very cold.
- DON'T let your diskettes get dusty.
- DON'T put diskettes near liquids and chemicals that may give off vapors.

What is the reason for all of these DON'Ts? Diskettes are like cassette tapes—you can record information on them and also play it back. Recording information is known as writing to the diskette; playing it back is known as reading the diskette. All of the things listed above can mar the surface of the diskette in such a way that your PC can no longer write or read information. A little carelessness and valuable information might be totally lost! If you take time to familiarize yourself with the DONT'S now, you can save yourself a lot of aggravation later on.

3 1/2-inch diskettes (see Figure 4.2) have a plastic jacket that protects the diskette from most of the dangers described above. A metal door covers the surface of the diskette for additional protection. The door slides open when the diskette is inside the drive, so that your PC can read information from and write information to the diskette. Even though 3 1/2-inch diskettes have more protection, they are still vulnerable. To prevent losing any information, pay attention to our list of DON'Ts—no matter what kind of diskette you are using.

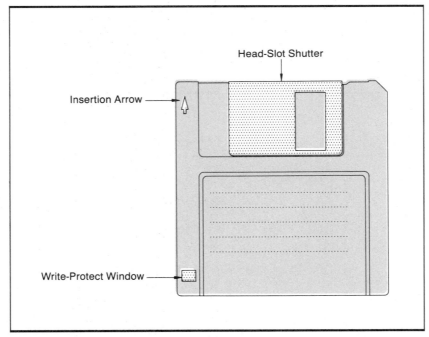

Figure 4.2: A 3 1/2-inch Diskette

Now we can talk about the DOs.

*L*abeling Diskettes

You will probably want to save related information on the same diskette, and it is useful to label each diskette with a general title. For example, if a diskette contains back-up copies of all of your reports for one sales region, an appropriate label is *Western Sales Region*. When pertinent, you might also include the date. Just as a book does not give all of its chapter titles on the cover, don't try to keep all the file names on the diskette label—the main subject is all you need. You can always get a complete file listing using the DIR command.

Diskette manufacturers provide sticky labels with each box of diskettes that you buy. Use them. Write the title on the label before you stick it on the diskette. If you want to change the title or write on the label after you have attached it to the diskette, use a felt-tip pen *only*. Ball-point pen and pencil are out—they can damage the diskette surface and make it unusable.

As shown in Figure 4.3, place the diskette label in the upper-right corner of the diskette next to the manufacturer's label (or in the upper part of a 3½-inch diskette). The labels are then all in one place for easy reference and storage. Be sure you do not put the label over any of the exposed surfaces—if you do, your PC will not be able to read from or write to the diskettes.

*S*toring Diskettes

Store your diskettes in a safe, easily accessible place. As the number of applications that you use and the amount of information that you have stored on diskette increase, storage becomes more and more of a concern.

Many manufacturers package software the same way that IBM does, in a plastic sleeve that fits in the back of the application reference binder. You can store the software diskette there, or you may want to keep all of your applications together in a storage container.

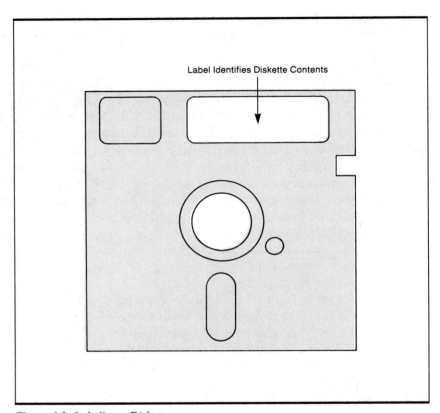

Figure 4.3: Labeling a Diskette

Several different kinds of diskette containers are available at computer stores or through other hardware and software vendors. Most offer some kind of filing divider and dust cover.

If you don't have a special diskette file, you can use the box you get when you buy diskettes. No matter how you store them, remember to use the paper sleeve they are delivered in. This protects them from dust and prevents you from accidentally touching the surface of the diskette.

Diskettes that contain highly sensitive or irreplaceable data should be stored even more carefully—under lock and key if necessary. Treat your computer software and stored documents just as you would any valuable document. In fact, go one step further and make a copy of any especially valuable diskettes.

Copying Diskettes

What if your computer malfunctions, or you delete something by mistake, or you simply lose a diskette? Things can go wrong, and they will. So get into the habit of backing up your software and information files.

Backing up means making a copy of the information stored on a diskette or hard disk. It protects you from losing information. You cannot appreciate the importance of adequate backup until you don't do it and wish you had. Most people don't bother at first, but sooner or later, they lose an important file. From that point on, they are always careful to make backup copies.

You can make a backup copy of all of the information on your hard disk, all information on a single diskette, or all information in a single file. You should develop your own backup procedure that includes all of these methods. Chapter 5 talks more about backing up in general. Right now, we are going to talk about copying an entire diskette, the procedure most useful for making backup copies of software programs. For example, you will want to make a copy of DOS.

Software manufacturers normally distribute applications on diskettes. You copy the program files from the diskettes to your hard disk, and use the hard disk version to run the program. The original diskettes are your backup. It is a good idea to copy the original diskettes as an extra precaution. You never know what might happen to them. (Some software manufacturers give you two copies of a program disk—one to copy to your hard disk and one for backup. Even if you have two disks, it is still a good idea to make a third.)

The manufacturers of some application software copy-protect their diskettes, which prevents you from copying them. However, you should always check your purchased software and make a backup copy if you can.

The DISKCOPY Command

Make a copy of the information on a diskette with the DISKCOPY command, which is part of DOS. DISKCOPY stands for *diskette copy*. You will need two diskettes: the diskette containing the information you want to copy, known to DOS as the *source diskette;* and a blank diskette, known to DOS as the *target diskette*, onto which the information will be copied.

The DISKCOPY command works only with diskette drives. You cannot use it to copy information to or from your hard disk. When you have just one diskette drive, you first copy information from the source diskette into the PC's memory, and then copy information from the PC's memory to the target diskette. The step-by-step procedure is outlined in the following list. If you have a two-drive system, you can copy information directly from one diskette to another. The procedure for using the DISKCOPY command with a two-drive system is explained in Appendix B.

1. Insert the DOS operating diskette in the diskette drive and close the drive door.

2. To begin copying the diskette, at the A> prompt type

   DISKCOPY ⏎

3. Your PC displays the message:

   Insert source diskette in drive A:
   Strike any key when ready

   Since you have already inserted the diskette, press any key to begin the copy operation.

4. The red drive light goes on and you hear a whirring sound. When the information on the diskette has been transferred into memory, you will see

   Insert target diskette in drive A:
   Strike any key when ready

5. Remove the DOS diskette, and return it to its protective sleeve.

6. Insert a blank diskette in the drive, close the drive door, and press any key to copy DOS onto this diskette.

Depending on the amount of memory available in your PC, you may have to repeat steps 1 and 3 through 6 more than once. If this is the case, DOS will tell you when to change diskettes.

7. Remove the backup copy of DOS from the drive. Before you put it away, take time to label it. Write "Backup Copy of DOS operating disk" on a label and add the version number that is on the original DOS diskette. Peel off the label and place it in the top right corner of the diskette. Return the diskette to its protective sleeve, and keep it nearby; we'll use it later. Store the original diskette in a safe place.

*W*rite-Protecting Diskettes

You need to be able to read all your diskettes, but you may not want to be able to write on some. For example, you probably will use the same diskettes over and over to back up important files. However you will not want to write on backup versions of application programs.

5 1/4-inch Diskettes

You can use a write-protect tab to prevent information from being added to or deleted from a 5 1/4-inch diskette.

Like labels, write-protect tabs are provided with diskettes when you buy them. They are small foil stickers that you place over the square notch on the side of the diskette. They are removable, so if you put a tab on a diskette to protect information that you do not want changed today, and tomorrow you decide that you want to change the information or overwrite the diskette, you can always take it off again.

Take a moment now to write-protect the copy of DOS that you made with the DISKCOPY command:

1. Remove a foil write-protect tab from the sheet of tabs provided with your diskettes.

2. Place the tab over the notch on the diskette as shown in Figure 4.4.

Now you are safe. No information can be added to or deleted from the diskette unless the tab is removed.

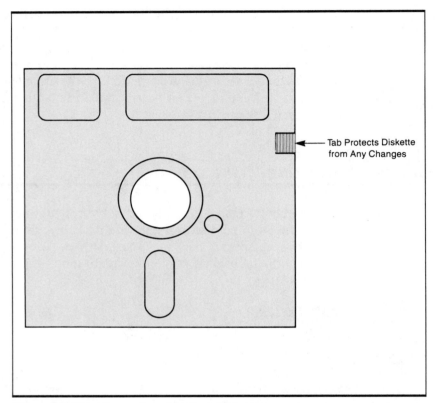

Figure 4.4: *Write-Protecting a 5 ¹/₄-inch Diskette*

3 ¹/₂-inch Diskettes

3 ¹/₂-inch diskettes have write-protect tabs built in. You protect the diskette by sliding the tab toward the edge of the diskette as shown in Figure 4.5. When a 3 ¹/₂-inch disk is write-protected, you can see through the hole that the tab covers.

Formatting a Diskette

When you *format* a diskette, you set the diskette to the recording format for DOS. Back to our stereo analogy again. If a record album

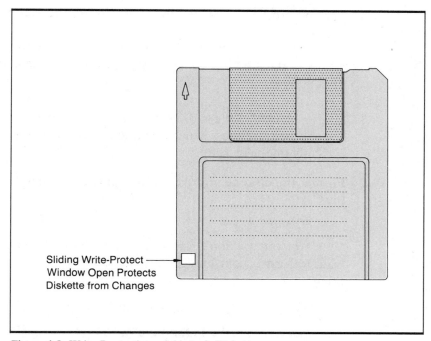

Sliding Write-Protect
Window Open Protects
Diskette from Changes

Figure 4.5: Write-Protecting a 3 ¹/₂-inch Diskette

has been recorded at 33 rpm and you play it back at 45 rpm, it sounds funny. Diskettes are somewhat the same except that they won't just sound funny; the computer won't be able to work with them at all. If the diskette has not been set to the format for DOS, you cannot even record information on it, let alone read it back.

Each operating system records information in its own format. When you format a diskette, you are indicating which format you are using. This means you do not have to buy different diskettes for different computers—you simply reformat and recycle them.

Formatting performs several operations: it sets the diskette to the correct recording format, checks the diskette for any defective areas that cannot receive information, and prepares the diskette to receive files. The result of all of this activity is a diskette that you can use to store information.

You did not need to format the diskette when you used the DISK-COPY command because your computer automatically formats the new diskette as part of that command. However, if you use a new diskette for any other purpose, you will have to use the FORMAT command first.

To format a diskette, use the FORMAT command followed by the drive identifier of the drive in which the new diskette is inserted. Take time to try it now.

1. Insert a blank diskette in drive A:. Make sure you use a blank diskette because the format operation overwrites anything currently on the diskette.

2. Format the diskette in drive A: by typing immediately after the C>:

   FORMAT A: ⏎

   Whatever you do, don't forget the A:, or DOS will think you want to format your hard disk (C:) and will wipe out everything on it.

3. Your computer helps you out with this message:

   Insert new diskette for drive A:
   and strike any key when ready

   Since you have already inserted the blank diskette, press any key to begin the formatting operation.

4. To let you know things are proceeding as planned, DOS sends you the message:

   Formatting . . .

   And when the operation is complete, it lets you know that, too:

   Formatting . . . format complete
   1213952 bytes total disk space
   1213952 total bytes available on disk
   Format another (Y/N)?

5. At this point you can remove the diskette from drive A:, insert another, type Y and continue formatting, or you can simply type N.

Checking Diskette Storage Space

Information is stored on diskettes in bytes. You can think of one byte as the amount of space needed to store one character. It is a little more complicated than that, but that's pretty much all you need to know for now.

The memory of your computer and the storage capacity of your diskettes are measured in thousands of bytes (called kilobytes or K bytes) or millions of bytes (called megabytes or M bytes). For example, a high-density diskette has 1.2 megabytes, the equivalent of approximately 600 double-spaced printed pages.

When you first start working with your PC, you will be tempted to use a separate diskette for each file that you need to store. This is great for diskette manufacturers and dealers, but probably not the most efficient use of your diskettes. You may fall into this habit because you are nervous about running out of diskette space—it is impossible to tell how much information you have stored on a diskette by looking at it. But don't worry; DOS can help you out with the CHKDSK command, which tells you how much diskette space you have left. (CHKDSK stands for *check disk*.)

The CHKDSK Command

The CHKDSK command can help you manage your diskettes to full advantage. If you want to copy a program or report onto a diskette that already contains some information, you can use CHKDSK to find out if there is enough room.

Use your backup copy of DOS and practice checking diskette space by following these steps:

1. Insert the diskette in drive A:, and close the drive door.

2. Check the status of the diskette, including available space, by typing at the C> prompt

   CHKDSK A: ⏎

   You receive a report that looks like this:

   362496   bytes total disk space
   0   bytes in 1 hidden files

> 319488   **bytes in 32 user files**
> 43008   **bytes available on disk**
>
> 655360   **bytes total memory**
> 601504   **bytes free**

As you can see, of the 362,496 bytes of storage on the diskette, 319,488 are used to store 32 files and 43,008 are available for storing additional information. (Your report will be slightly different.)

In addition, your computer tells you a bit about itself; of the 655,360 bytes of space in its memory, 53,856 are being used and hence 601,504 bytes are free. Those 53,856 bytes are taken up by DOS. (Again, the numbers for your PC will be different.) When you use an application program such as Lotus 1-2-3, you load that program into memory, too. The remaining memory is used as temporary storage for the reports or documents you are using with the application program.

3. You can also use the CHKDSK command to report the amount of space available on your hard disk. At the C> prompt, type:

CHKDSK ⟵

You see a report like the following one:

> 32010240   **bytes total disk space**
> 49152   **bytes in 3 hidden files**
> 157696   **bytes in 72 directories**
> 17164288   **bytes in 1036 user files**
> 14639104   **bytes available on disk**
>
> 655360   **bytes total memory**
> 601504   **bytes free**

This report is for a hard disk that has many files stored on it. Your hard disk probably has very few. It tells you that there are 32,010,240 bytes of storage on the disk. Of the available storage, 49,152 bytes are used to store hidden files; hidden files are files that DOS alone uses. 157,696 bytes are used to store information about directories, which are described in Chapter 5. 17,164,288 bytes are used to store your files, and 14,639,104 bytes are available for storing new files.

*C*leaning Diskette Drives

Diskette drives should be cleaned on a regular basis, depending on the amount of time you use your PC. Keeping the environment as free from dust as possible and cleaning your diskette drive are important maintenance steps.

The easiest way to clean the drives is with purchased cleaning kits which are available, with other computer supplies, at computer dealers. Each kit includes instructions for proper use, and usually either a pretreated fabric diskette or one that you treat with a cleaning solution. (Use only the cleaner provided in the kit.)

Turn on your PC, insert the cleaning diskette into the drive, and close the door. Leave it in for about a minute and then remove it. It's as simple as that!

Here is a quick review of this chapter; then we will tell you how to set up a filing system on your hard disk.

*R*eview

Diskettes:

- Are used to store information.
- Can be written to and read from.
- Can be write-protected by covering the write notch with a special tab (5¹/₄-inch diskettes) or by sliding the built-in tab toward the edge of the diskette (3¹/₂-inch diskettes).
- Must be handled with care.

When using diskettes:

- Label for easy reference.
- Store in a safe, dust-free spot.
- Back up all information.
- Do not write on the diskettes surface.

The DISKCOPY command:

- Copies all the information from one diskette to another.
- Does not copy to or from a hard disk.

The FORMAT command:

- Prepares a diskette for use.
- Warning: Never unintentionally format your hard disk.

The CHKDSK command:

- Checks the space on the diskette or hard disk in the designated drive.
- Displays a status report that includes the amount of free space on the disk and in the PC's memory.

Cleaning the diskette drives:

- Do on a regular basis depending on frequency of use.
- Use a purchased cleaning kit.

5

Building a
Filing System

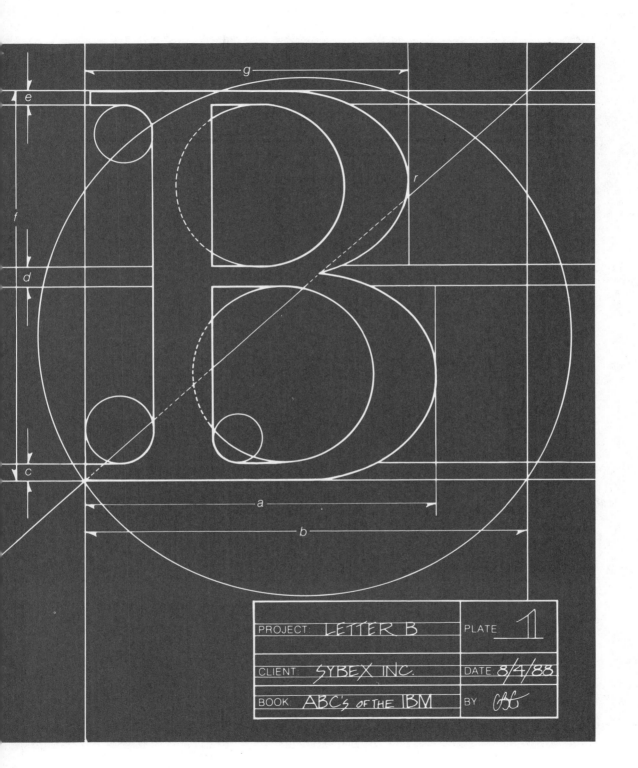

PROJECT: LETTER B   PLATE 1

CLIENT: SYBEX INC.   DATE 8/4/88

BOOK: ABC's OF THE IBM   BY CBS

All the information you store in your IBM PC is organized in files on your hard disk and on diskettes. As you acquire application programs and use them to create letters, reports, worksheets, and other documents, you will accumulate many files. In fact, you can store thousands of files on one hard disk. To keep track of all of these files, you can organize them into a filing system. Just as you organize paper files in folders in file cabinets, you organize your PC's files in directories on your hard disk.

If you think of your PC's hard disk as a filing cabinet, a *directory* is like a folder in that cabinet. It is a place for storing files that are related to each other in some way. For example, if you do word processing for several departments within your company, you might create a directory for each department. You would store the documents you create for a particular department in its directory. You use a directory's name as you might use a label on a folder to remind you what files are stored in it.

Diskettes can also have directories; however, because of the way that you use them and the amount of information you store on them, you rarely need to set up directories on diskettes. Throughout this chapter, we will assume that you are building a filing system on your hard disk.

Designing Your Filing System

DOS automatically creates the first directory on a hard disk or diskette for you. It is called the *root directory*, because, if you think of the directory structure as a tree with many branches (see Figure 5.1), the first directory is like the root of the tree. All other directories branch off from it. You use the backslash (\) symbol to designate the root directory.

Within the root directory, you might create separate directories for different types of information. For example, you might have one directory in which you keep sales reports, one for sales plans, and one for expenses. Technically, these directories are called *subdirectories* because they exist within another directory (the root).

You can create as many subdirectories as you want within a directory, and directories can contain both files and subdirectories. For example, in

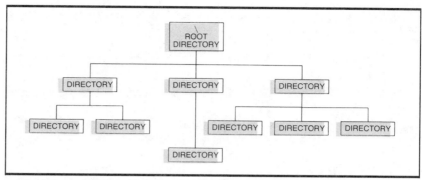

Figure 5.1: *The Directory Structure*

the expenses directory, you might have a directory for each region. Within the directory for a particular region, you may keep a database file containing information about each salesperson and a directory for each salesperson that contains expense account files.

You can work in any directory you want. The directory in which you are working is called the *current directory*. Just as you can make drive C: or drive A: your current drive, you can make any directory your current directory. We will show you how to do this later in this chapter. From the current directory, you can work with files in any directory. We will also talk more about using files with commands later in this chapter.

Take some time now to start thinking about how you might organize your filing system. We will give you the commands to actually set up your filing system later in this chapter. Don't let your directory structure get so complicated that you can't remember where files are. If you do forget, use the DIR command to list the files in different directories until you find the file you want.

Most application programs recommend that you install them in their own directories. You may want to store information created with these programs in the application directories or in directories with names that are more meaningful to you. You can design your filing system in any way you want, and usually no two systems are the same. However, if other people will use your PC, you may want to consult them before you develop your system.

*A*ssigning Directory Names

Each subdirectory within a directory is identified by a unique name. Whenever possible, choose names that reflect the information stored in the subdirectory. For example, SALESRPT is a good name for a sales report directory.

*R*ules for Directory Names

A directory name must be between one and eight characters long. It can consist of letters, numbers, or symbols. However, it must begin with a letter and cannot contain a period, asterisk, a question mark, a space, or any of the following symbols: < > : ; =] [.
Here are some directory names that follow the rules:

ACCTSPAY

LETTERS

BUDGETS

NEWSLTTR

Here are some names that are not allowed:

JAN.RPTS	(includes a period)
1988STMT	(begins with a number)
JOY WONG	(has a space)
FEBRECORDS	(exceeds eight characters)

*C*reating a Directory

Use the MKDIR command to create a new subdirectory. MKDIR stands for *make directory*. You type MKDIR and the directory's name.
The root directory is the current directory on drive C:. Let's create a subdirectory within it for storing example files.

1. Make drive C: the current drive. After the A> prompt, type

    C:←

2. Immediately after C>, type

    MKDIR EXAMPLES ←

In Chapter 3, you used the DIR command to list the files on the DOS diskette. DIR lists all of the files and subdirectories within a directory. Because the DOS diskette has only one directory, the root, you listed all the files on the diskette when you used DIR in Chapter 3. When the list you get from using the DIR command contains directories, DOS displays <DIR> after each directory name so that you can distinguish directories from files.

Now, use the DIR command to check for the new directory.

3. Immediately after C>, type

    DIR ←

    You see a list of the files and directories in the root directory. In the list, you should see:

    EXAMPLES <DIR> 3-28-89 12:01p

Figure 5.2 shows the directory structure for your hard disk.

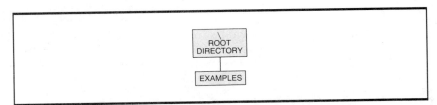

Figure 5.2: Your Hard Disk's Directory Structure

Changing the Current Directory

Your hard disk now has at least two directories: the root directory and the EXAMPLES directory you created. When you first start up your PC, the root directory is the current directory. The current directory is sometimes also called the *working directory* because it is the directory in which you are currently working.

You use the CHDIR command to change the current directory. CHDIR stands for *change directory*. You might change the current directory to an application directory before you use that application. The advantage of changing the current directory is that it is easier to work with files when they are in the current directory. We will say more about working with files later.

Practice changing the current directory.

1. To make EXAMPLES the current directory, type

    CHDIR EXAMPLES ⏎

2. To learn which directory is the current directory, type

    CHDIR ⏎

    DOS tells you the name for the current directory:

    C:\EXAMPLES

3. Now make a subdirectory within the EXAMPLES directory and name it SUB1. After the C>, type

    MKDIR SUB1 ⏎

4. Let's make a second subdirectory and call it SUB2. After the C>, type

    MKDIR SUB2 ⏎

Figure 5.3 shows the new directory structure for your PC.

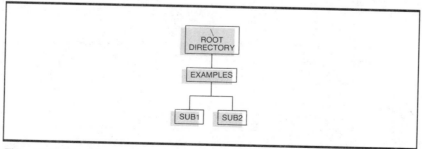

Figure 5.3: *New Directory Structure*

5. Make SUB1 the current directory. Type

    CHDIR SUB1 ⏎

6. Now, check the current directory. Type

   CHDIR ⏎

   You should see:

   C:\EXAMPLES\SUB1

But you named the new directory SUB1. What's all this other other information DOS is giving you? DOS is telling you the *path name* for the directory. The path name tells you exactly where the directory belongs in your filing system. In this case, the path name tells you that the directory SUB1 is located in the examples directory, which is located within the root directory on drive C:.

Using Path Names for Directories

You can think of a path name as a directory's full name. DOS uses path names to distinguish directories with similar names. You might use a person's full name in a similar way. For example, you might have a co-worker named Phillip Smith. Although you probably call him Phillip or Phil, in your company's employee records he is known by his full name, Phillip A. Smith. Using his full name distinguishes him from any other employees named Phillip or even Phillip Smith.

The DOS path name tells you exactly where the directory is located in your filing system. It includes the name of the drive on which the directory is located, the list of directories through which DOS must search to find the directory, and finally the directory name. A backslash character (\) separates each element of the path name. The backslash between the drive identifier and the first directory represents the root directory.

Figure 5.4 shows how you determine the path name for the directory SUB1.

You use a directory's path name with a command to tell DOS exactly which directory you want to use. You can always use the complete path name; however, there are two useful shortcuts:

- If the directory you want to use is on the current drive, you can leave the drive identifier out of the path name. For

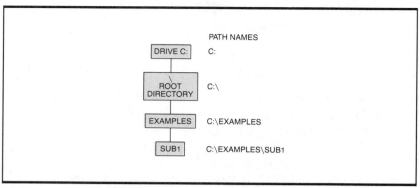

Figure 5.4: A Directory's Path Name

example, since SUB1 is on the current drive, you can shorten its path name to the following:

\EXAMPLES\SUB1

- If the subdirectory is in the current directory, you can leave out all parts of the path name that tell DOS how to get to the current directory. You used this shortcut when you created the EXAMPLES directory.

You will find that using these shortcuts saves you a lot of typing. If you use one of the shortcuts and the command doesn't work as you expected, try the command again, but this time use the full path name.

*R*emoving a Directory

When would you want to remove an entire directory? Suppose you set up a directory for information for a project. You might have several files in the directory. When the project is complete, you may no longer need to keep the files on your hard disk. You can copy the files to diskettes and delete the directory.

You use the RMDIR command to remove a directory. RMDIR stands for *remove directory*. You must remove all of the files from a directory before you can delete the directory. Before deleting files, you should always copy them to a diskette just in case you need them again sometime. We'll show you how to copy and delete files later in this chapter.

Let's remove one of the directories we created earlier.

1. Type

    RMDIR \EXAMPLES\SUB2 ↵

    You must type the path name because SUB2 is not a subdirectory within the current directory. However, because drive C: is the current drive, you do not need to include the drive identifier. (Remember, C:\EXAMPLES\SUB1 is the current directory.)

2. Now, check that DOS removed the SUB2 directory. Type

    DIR \EXAMPLES ↵

    This command tells DOS to list all of the directories and files in the EXAMPLES directory. Because EXAMPLES is not the current directory, you must give its path name. Make sure that SUB2 is not listed.

You create directories in order to organize your files. All of the information in your PC exists in files. Both the programs you use and the information you create with them exist in files. We will spend the rest of this chapter describing how you work with and back up files.

*A*ssigning File Names

Each file within a directory is identified by a unique name. Whenever possible, choose names that reflect the information stored in the file. For example, TESTPLAN is probably the best name anyone could come up with for a file containing a product test plan. What if you forget the exact name of a file? Don't worry—you can always list all the files stored in a directory with the DIR command.

*R*ules for File Names

You normally assign a file name when you create the file in an application program or when you copy a file with DOS. File names follow the same rules as directory names. A file name must be between one and eight characters long. It can consist of letters, numbers, or symbols. However, it must begin with a letter and cannot contain a period, asterisk, a question mark, a space, or any of the following symbols: < > : ; =] [.

Obviously, as you accumulate more and more files, you will find it harder to come up with unique, meaningful names when you have only eight characters to play with. To overcome this problem, you have the option of tagging something called an *extension* onto the end of the file name. Extensions can consist of a period followed by one to three characters. You can use them to identify the type of information in the file. For example, you could use the extension .LET to identify letters, or the extension .DOC for documents. If you give a file name an extension, you must include it any time you refer to the file.

Some application programs use extensions to distinguish different types of files, whereas program files are followed by an extension that identifies the language in which they are written. For example, the 1-2-3 spreadsheet program uses the extension .WK1 for spreadsheets and the extension .PIC for graphs. BASIC program files have the extension .BAS. These extensions are added automatically to the file name when you save the file. You do not have to enter them with the file name.

DOS also uses extensions to designate different types of files. For a complete description of DOS file extensions, refer to your DOS reference manual.

Here are some file names that obey the rules:

REGION3
SALESRPT.86
INCMSTMT.WK1
REDINC.LET

These files do not obey the rules:

1STFILE	(begins with a number)
MAIL LIST	(includes a space)
JONES ACCOUNT	(exceeds eight characters, includes a space)
MR.SMITH	(includes a period—SMITH is not a valid extension)

When you begin naming files, adopt some kind of a system. If most of your work is word processing, you may want to store all documents for a particular account in the same directory and follow a convention for naming letters, proposals, and project reports. If you frequently do reports with a spreadsheet program, you might want them all in one directory also, but since the directory would then include data for many clients, you would want to name the report files so that you could easily identify the client to which a particular report belongs.

*U*sing Path Names for Files

Suppose you had organized your hard disk into directories for each of four sales regions and you were about to use a spreadsheet program to develop the sales plans for each region. Would you have to come up with a different file name for each sales plan? No. Because the files for the sales plans are in different directories, they can each have the same name—for example, SALESPLN.WK1. Figure 5.5 shows this file organization.

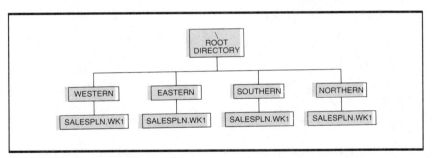

Figure 5.5: Sample File System

To DOS, the files are unique because they have different path names. Like a directory's path name, a file's path name tells its exact location in your file system. It includes the name of the drive on which the file is located, the list of directories through which DOS must search to find the file, and finally the file name. A backslash character (\) separates each element of the path name. The backslash between the drive name and the first directory represents the root directory.

The path names for the sales plans in the example would be

C:\WESTERN\SALESPLN.WK1
C:\EASTERN\SALESPLN.WK1
C:\SOUTHERN\SALESPLN.WK1
C:\NORTHERN\SALESPLN.WK1

You can see that each path name is unique. You use path names with commands to tell DOS exactly which file or directory you want to use. You can use the same shortcuts that you use for directory path names for file path names:

- If the file you want to name is on the current drive, you can leave the drive name out of the path name.

- If the file is in the current directory, you can leave out all parts of the path name that tell DOS how to get to the current directory.

If you request a file without giving DOS enough information to find it, you receive the message

File not found

All you need to do is retype the command using the file's complete path name.

*W*ild Card Characters

In a card game, a wild card can represent any card in the deck. DOS has two wild card characters, the asterisk (*) and the question mark (?). An (*) in a file name or extension means that any character can fill that position and any remaining positions in the name or extension. A (?) in a file name or extension means that any character can fill that position only.

Once you start to build a system of directories containing many files, you will find wild card characters an easy way to work with groups of file names. For example, you can list a group of files, perhaps all files with the letter M, or all files with the extension .BAS.

Here's how wild card characters work.

1. Insert the duplicate DOS operating diskette that you made in Chapter 4 in drive A:. (We use the DOS diskette for our examples because we don't know exactly which files you have on your hard disk.)

2. Use * to list all files on the DOS diskette beginning with M. Immediately after C>, type

   DIR A:M* ⏎

Your PC lists the files on the DOS diskette that begin with M. (Our version of DOS has two files that begin with M; yours may have more.)

3. To list all files with the extension .EXE, type

   DIR A:*.EXE ⏎

If your copy of DOS is the same as ours, this command lists nine files, all with the extension .EXE.

4. Try using a ? to list all files that are named BASIC or BASIC followed by another character. Type

   DIR A:BASIC? ⏎

Four file names are listed on our copy of DOS:

> **BASIC   COM**
> **BASICA   COM**
> **BASIC   DIF**
> **BASICA   DIF**

If there were a file named BASICAL on the DOS diskette, it would not be listed with the ?—you would have to use *.

Copying Files

You have already used the DISKCOPY command to copy an entire diskette. Often you will want to copy only a single file or group of files, not the whole diskette. That is what the COPY command is for. When you copy a file, you do just that—copy it. It is like using your office copier. The original remains intact, but you now have a duplicate.

Making a Copy on Another Disk

Why would you copy a file from one disk to another? One reason is to back up your work. Making a copy of a file on a second disk means you have a duplicate of the file for safety. Normally, you back up files on your hard disk by copying them to a diskette. There are also lots of other reasons for copying files from one disk to another. Most software manufacturers distribute application programs on diskettes. Since you will want to keep all of your applications on your hard disk, you must copy the program from the diskette to the hard disk. (The process of installing an application on your hard disk may involve more than just copying files; be sure to follow the software manufacturer's instructions.) You may also use diskettes to share information with co-workers. For example, a co-worker might give you a diskette containing standard letters for responding to different customer requests. Before you modify these letters for particular customers, you may want to copy them to your hard disk.

We will assume that you still have the duplicate DOS diskette in drive A: and that C:\EXAMPLES\SUB1 is the current directory. We are going to copy the file TREE.COM from the diskette in drive A: to a new file called OAK.COM in the current directory:

1. Immediately after C>, type

   COPY A:TREE.COM OAK.COM ↵

You do not need to include a path for the duplicate file because you are copying it to the current directory. Because you are giving it a new name, you must supply the name and the extension.

When it has finished the copying operation, DOS gives you the message:

   1 File(s) copied

2. Now let's copy TREE.COM from DOS in drive A: to a new file with the same name in the current directory of drive C:. Immediately after C>, type:

   COPY A:TREE.COM ↵

You must give the full path name for the file on drive A:. Because you want the copy in the current directory to have the same name as the original, you do not have to give DOS a new name. When copying is complete, you will see the same message as before on your screen.

3. Want to try an example with wild card characters? To copy all files beginning with the letter R from the diskette in drive A: to the EXAMPLES directory on drive C:, type

    COPY A:R∗.∗ C:\EXAMPLES ←┘

Something new happens here. When you use wild cards to copy multiple files, DOS lists the name of each file as it copies them so that you know what you are getting. At the end of the copy operation, the message on your screen looks like this:

RECOVER.COM
REPLACE.EXE
RESTORE.COM
3 File(s) copied

When you use the ∗ wild card in this way, you need to type an ∗ for the file extension as well as the file name. Typing COPY R∗ would not have copied any files, since all files beginning with R on the DOS diskette have extensions. Remember, when a file has an extension, you must use it whenever you use the file name.

*M*aking a Copy in Another Directory

Suppose you keep all the documents related to each of your clients in separate directories. You need to write a letter to Mr. Jones and you remember that last month you wrote a similar letter to Ms. Smith. Instead of typing the letter all over again, you can copy the letter from Ms. Smith's directory to Mr. Jones' directory and make whatever changes are necessary, thereby saving yourself a lot of typing.

Let's practice copying a file from one directory to another by copying TREE.COM from C:\EXAMPLES\SUB1 to C:EXAMPLES. We are assuming that C:\EXAMPLES\SUB1 is still your current directory.

1. Immediately after C>, type

    COPY TREE.COM \EXAMPLES ←┘

You do not have to include the full path name for the original file because it is in the current directory. Because you are using the same file name, you do not have to give a name for the duplicate in the EXAMPLES directory.

2. Now copy TREE.COM from the EXAMPLES directory to a file called WILLOW in the current directory. Type

COPY \EXAMPLES\TREE.COM WILLOW ↵

You have to give DOS the full path name for the original file because it is not in the current directory. You give a new name only for the duplicate file. Its path is not required because you are copying it to the current directory.

*M*aking a Copy in the Same Directory

Suppose you produce a monthly report. Instead of redoing the whole report each month, you can simply make a copy of last month's report, update the copy in a few places, and store it as this month's report. If you used the original rather than a copy, you would no longer have a report for last month!

When you copy a file within a directory, you must give the copy a different file name—DOS will not let you have more than one file with the same name in a directory. So, for example, the copy of a file named SALESRPT might be called SALESRPT.CPY.

If you want to copy a file in the current drive and directory, you do not need to give the drive name and directory name in the path name. You simply give the name of the original file followed by a space and the name of the duplicate file.

Let's try making a copy of the file WILLOW in the current directory. We will call the copy PINE.

Type

COPY WILLOW PINE ↵

You see the message:

1 File(s) copied

If you need proof that your PC did as you asked, check the directory by typing

    DIR ←—

There should now be a file named PINE at the end of the list.

At this point, remove the DOS diskette from drive A: and store it in a safe place.

*R*enaming a File

What if you think of a better name for a file, or want to change the name to be consistent with other file names? You can always change the name of a file with the RENAME command. You give the current name of the file and the name you want to change it to. It's that simple. The next time you want to look for the file, use its new name. Nothing in the file will change—only the name will be different.

In an earlier exercise, we copied the file TREE.COM from the DOS diskette in drive A: to the current directory on drive C: (C:\EXAMPLES\SUB1). We called the copy OAK. Now we have decided that the name OAK is not descriptive enough and that the name NEWTREE would suit us better. Let's rename the file.

1. Immediately after C>, type

    RENAME OAK NEWTREE ←—

2. DOS does not give you any message to confirm the change, but you can check that things went smoothly with the DIR command. Type

    DIR ←—

There should now be a file called NEWTREE in the SUB1 directory. If OAK had been in a directory other than the current directory, you would have had to use its full path name to identify it.

*E*rasing or Deleting a File

If you no longer need a file, you can delete it with either the ERASE command or the DEL command. Both do the same thing. The important thing to remember with these commands is that once a file has been deleted, it is gone—there is no getting it back. So be sure you know what the file contains before you delete it.

All you need to do to delete a file is give the command followed by the path name. As always, the path name includes the drive identifier, the necessary directory names, and an extension when they apply.

1. Let's delete the file NEWTREE in the current directory of drive C:. Immediately after C>, type

   DEL NEWTREE ⏎

Since NEWTREE is in the current directory, we need only type the file name.

2. Use the DIR command to check that the file has been deleted.

3. Earlier on we created a file named PINE in the current directory. Let's erase that file now. Immediately after C>, type

   ERASE PINE ⏎

4. Are you ready to use the wild card character * to delete a couple of files at once? If you remember, we still have copies of the DOS files RECOVER.COM, REPLACE.EXE, and RESTORE.COM in the EXAMPLES directory. Delete them by typing immediately after the C>:

   DEL \EXAMPLES R*.* ⏎

Be very careful when using * to erase files. You do not want to lose more than you planned. You could in fact delete all the files in a directory by typing the ERASE or DEL command with *.*. In response, DOS would give you the opportunity for second thoughts by asking: **Are you sure (Y/N)?** If you know what you are doing, type Y; if not, you can cancel the operation by typing N. Isn't it nice to know DOS doesn't trust you as much as you trust yourself?

Let's delete all the files in the two directories, EXAMPLES and SUB1, that we created earlier.

1. Type

   CHDIR \ ⏎

2. Next delete all of the files in the SUB1 directory. Type

   DEL EXAMPLES\SUB1 *.* ⏎

3. DOS asks you if you are sure you want to delete all of the files in a directory. Type Y. If you want to cancel the command, you would type N.

4. Now delete the files in the EXAMPLES directory. Type

   ERASE EXAMPLES *.* ←

5. When DOS asks if you are sure you want to delete all of the files in the directory, type Y.

6. Type

   DIR ←

*B*acking Up Your File System

Backing up your file system means making a copy of the information stored on your hard disk. You will invest a lot of time in installing application programs, setting up directories, and creating files on your hard disk. You can protect a single file by copying it onto a diskette, but the only way you can protect all of your files and your directory structure is by backing up your hard disk. Backing up your disk regularly protects you from wasting your effort and losing your information.

You should begin by establishing a regular schedule for performing complete and incremental backups. A complete backup copies all of the directories and files on your hard disk. If you have a lot of information stored in your file system, a complete backup can take a long time. An incremental backup copies the directories and files that have changed since the last complete backup.

How often you should perform a complete backup depends on how often you use your PC and how important your files are. For most people, weekly complete backups with daily incremental backups are adequate. Others may not need to perform backups as often. People who use their PC heavily may want to perform a complete backup every day.

*B*ackup Methods

There are several ways to perform backups. You can choose from several forms of backup media. You might use diskettes, tape cartridges, or cartridge disks. To use any media other than diskettes, however, you must purchase additional hardware. DOS gives you commands for backing up to diskettes and tape. There are also several backup programs available from software manufacturers. These programs can be faster and easier to use than DOS commands. We will describe how to back up your hard disk using DOS commands and diskettes since these methods are available to all PC owners. This method can be very time-consuming compared to using other media and other programs; therefore, we recommend that you investigate other options if you have a lot of files to back up.

*U*sing the Backup Command

To perform a complete backup of your hard disk,

1. Change your current directory to the root directory. After C>, type

    CHDIR \ ←

2. Use the BACKUP command to tell DOS to back up all files in the current directory and all of its subdirectories from drive C: to drive A:. After the C>, type

    BACKUP C: A:/S ←

    You see the following message:

    > **Insert backup diskette 01 in drive A:**
    > **Warning! Files in the target drive**
    > **A:\ root directory will be erased**
    > **Strike any key when ready**

3. Insert a formatted diskette in drive A:. Be sure to use a disk that does not contain any valuable information. Press any key. DOS begins backing up files. You see the following message:

    > *** * * Backing up files to drive A: * * ***
    > **Diskette Number: 01**

DOS lists the path name for each file it backs up. This is a good time to take a coffee break or make a few phone calls. It can take 15 to 20 minutes to fill a diskette. When the first diskette is full, you see the following message:

> **Insert backup diskette 02 in drive A:**
> **Warning! Files in the target drive**
> **A:\ root directory will be erased**
> **Strike any key when ready**

4. Remove the first diskette from drive A:. Write BACKUP DISKETTE 1 and the date on a label, and place the label on the diskette. It is important to label and number your backup diskettes. If you need to restore files to your system from them, you must use them in order.

5. Insert a new diskette in drive A: and press any key to continue the backup. DOS tells you that it is continuing with the backup and lists the files backed up.

6. When the second diskette is full, label it and insert a new one. Continue following DOS's instructions to insert new diskettes until the backup is complete. You know that the backup is complete when you see the C> prompt.

You can also use the BACKUP command to back up only those files that have changed since the last complete backup.

1. Change your current directory to the root directory. After C>, type

> **CHDIR \ ↵**

2. Use the /S and /M parameters with the BACKUP command. After the C>, type

> **BACKUP C: A:/S/M ↵**

The /M at the end of this command tells DOS to back up only the files that have changed since the last backup. It backs up all files in the current directory and all of its subdirectories from drive C: to drive A:. You see the following message:

> **Insert backup diskette 01 in drive A:**
> **Warning! Files in the target drive**

A:\ root directory will be erased
Strike any key when ready

3. Insert a formatted diskette in drive A:. Be sure to use a disk that does not contain any valuable information. Press any key. DOS begins backing up files. You see the following message:

* * * Backing up files to drive A: * * *
Diskette Number: 01

DOS lists the path name for each file it backs up.

4. If necessary, insert additional disks when DOS asks for them. Be sure to label each disk with its number, the date, and INCREMENTAL BACKUP. When the backup is complete, you see the C> prompt.

Using the RESTORE Command

We hope you will never have to use your backup files. However, things can go wrong. For example, you might accidentally delete an important file. You use the RESTORE command to copy files from your backup diskettes to your hard disk. We show you how to restore files in this chapter. Because you do not need to restore files at the moment, just read through the procedure now. Reread it when you actually need to restore files.

1. Find the diskettes from your last complete backup.

2. With the RESTORE command, you give DOS the complete path names for the files you want to RESTORE. Of course, you can also use wild card characters. Let's assume that you accidentally deleted all the files in a directory named NEWACCTS, and now you want to copy them from your backup diskettes. You would type

RESTORE A: C:\NEWACCTS *.* ↵

This command tells DOS to restore all files in the NEWACCT directory from drive A: to drive C:. You see the following message:

Insert backup diskette 01 in drive A:
Strike any key when ready

3. Insert the first backup diskette in drive A:, then press any key. You must copy files from the backup diskettes in order. You see another message:

* * * Files were backed up 03/03/89 * * *
* * Restoring files from drive A: * * *

DOS lists the names of the files as it restores them. When it completes restoring the files from the first backup diskette or if it does not find the files you want on the first diskette, DOS asks you to insert the second diskette.

4. Continue to insert the backup diskettes into drive A: as DOS asks for them. The restoration is complete when you see the C> prompt.

5. Now restore the files from your last incremental backup. Follow the procedure in steps 1 through 4, but use the diskettes from the incremental backup. DOS will only replace the files on the incremental backup disks.

In this chapter, we have covered a lot of information that you will use on a regular basis. So here is a quick review to refer back to as you begin using your PC on your own.

*R*eview

Filing system:

- Consists of directories and files.
- DOS creates the first directory, called the *root*, automatically.
- The \ symbol designates the root directory.
- A directory can have any number of *subdirectories*, and its subdirectories can have their own subdirectories.

Directory and subdirectory names:

- Each subdirectory within a directory must have a unique name.

- Directory names can be one to eight characters long and must begin with a letter.
- Directory names cannot include a period, space, asterisk, or question mark.

Path names:

- You must use path names with commands to tell DOS exactly which file or directory you want to use.
- The path name for a file consists of its drive identifier, a \ for the root directory, a list of all of the directories through which DOS much search to find the file with directory names separated by a \, and the file name including the extension.
- The path name for a directory consists of its drive identifier, a \ for the root directory, a list of all of the directories through which DOS much search to find the file with directory names separated by a \, and the name of the directory you want to use.
- When the file or directory you want to use is on the current disk, you can omit the drive identifier from the path name.
- When the file or directory you want to use is in the current directory or one of its subdirectories, you can omit all of the information in the path name that tells DOS how to get to the current directory.

The MKDIR command:

- Creates a new directory.

The CHDIR command:

- Changes the current directory to the directory you name.
- Reports the name of the current directory if you don't name a directory.

The RMDIR command:

- Removes a directory from your disk.
- Only works if you first delete all files from the directory.

File names:

- Each file in a subdirectory must have a unique name.

- A file name can be one to eight characters long and must begin with a letter.

- You cannot include a period, space, asterisk, or question mark in a file name.

File extensions:

- A file extension is a three-character identifier separated from the file name by a period. (It can be less than three characters, but not more.)

- If a file name has an extension, you must include the extension when you use the file name.

Wild card characters:

- An asterisk in a file name or extension means that any character can fill that position and any remaining positions in the name.

- A question mark in a file name or extension means that any single character can fill that position only.

The COPY command:

- Is used to make a copy of a file on another disk, in another directory, or in the same directory. You can give the copy either the same name as the original or a new name.

- Can be used with wild card characters to copy several files at once.

The RENAME command:

- Renames a file.

The DEL or ERASE command:

- Deletes a file.

Backing up your hard disk:

- Saves the information and effort in your file system.

- Requires a regular schedule of complete and incremental backups.

- Is accomplished with any of a variety of backup media and backup programs.

- Use the BACKUP command to perform backups to diskette.

- Use the RESTORE command to copy files from backup diskettes to your hard disk.

6

Computer Applications: Tools for Your PC

Featuring

Installing, backing up, and loading an application

Entering, saving, retrieving, revising, and printing information

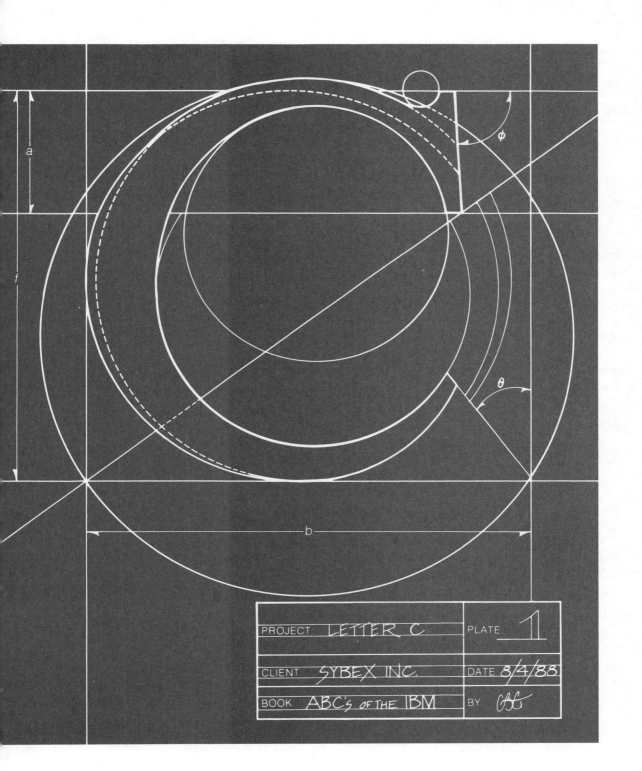

PROJECT: LETTER C   PLATE: 1

CLIENT: SYBEX INC.   DATE 8/4/88

BOOK: ABC's OF THE IBM   BY:

So I know about diskettes and files and DOS commands and menus and function keys, you are saying. *What happens now?* Well, this is the moment you've been waiting for! We are going to talk about application programs, the tools that put your computer to work for you.

Application programs take personal computers out of the domain of the technical expert and turn them into useful and productive tools for everyone. The majority of people use their PCs with application programs selected to meet their particular needs. So this chapter introduces you to applications. You will see that all our rules about disks and files are for good reason. Any application you use relies on disks to store your information and file names to identify the information you want to work with. Before you purchase an application, be sure you can use it with your PC. Some applications require additional memory or a special monitor or adapter.

Installing an Application

The process of copying an application program from the diskette on which it is distributed to your hard disk is called *installing* the application. The application program may consist of one or more files, and the diskette on which it is distributed may contain different versions of files for different types of PCs. Often, you must create a special directory on the hard disk for the application. For these reasons, it does not make sense to install an application by simply copying all of the files from the distribution diskette to your hard disk.

Follow the software manufacturer's instructions for installing an application program. Sometimes applications come with programs that copy the appropriate files for you. All you do is answer questions that the program asks about your system.

In Chapter 7 we will introduce you to two applications, a word processor and a financial spreadsheet. We use the two currently most popular programs, WordPerfect and Lotus 1-2-3. If you have these two programs, install them on your PC now. If you do not, install the word processing and spreadsheet programs you have; you may be able to follow many of our instructions anyway.

*M*aking a Backup Copy

As we said in Chapter 4, it is a good practice to make a backup of your important diskettes. This is just as true for application program diskettes as it is for DOS and your information files. Once you have installed an application, you should make a copy of it. Store the duplicate and the original diskette in a safe place. If anything ever happens to the installed version, you can always make another copy from the original or the duplicate.

However, as with every rule, there are exceptions to always backing up, since some application program diskettes are copy-protected. This means that the manufacturer has made the diskette in a special way that prevents it from being copied. They usually label these diskettes *Copy Protected* so you will know whether you can copy them or not. Often they give you a backup diskette so that you do not have to create your own. In short, if you can copy your application program diskette, you should do so.

1. Turn on your PC, if it is not on already.

2. To begin copying the diskette, at the A> prompt type

   DISKCOPY

3. Your PC displays the message:

   Insert SOURCE diskette in drive A:
   Press any key when ready . . .
   Copying 40 tracks
   9 sectors/Track, 2 Side(s)

4. Insert the application diskette in drive A: and press any key to begin the copy operation.

5. The red drive light goes on and you hear a whirring sound. When the information on the diskette has been transferred into memory, you see

   Insert TARGET diskette in drive A:
   Press any key when ready . . .

6. Remove the application diskette.

7. Insert a blank diskette in the drive, close the drive door, and press any key to copy the application files onto this diskette.

Depending on the amount of memory available in your PC, you may have to repeat steps 4 through 7 more than once. If this is the case, DOS will tell you when to change diskettes.

8. Remove the backup copy of the application from the drive. Before you put it away, take time to label it. Return both diskettes to their protective sleeves, and store them in a safe place.

Loading an Application Program

After you have installed an application program, you load it whenever you want to use it. To load an application program

1. Change the current directory to the application directory. The software manufacturer's installation instructions usually recommend a name for the application directory, but you can name it whatever you want.

2. Type the program name. Refer to the software manufacturer's instructions for the correct program name.

3. Press ←⏎.

Using an Application Program

All application programs are unique—even those intended for the same purpose work in different ways. Nonetheless, you will perform some typical operations, no matter what application you are using. We are going to introduce you to a few of these now.

Depending on your application, you will give commands, choose menu items, or use predefined function keys to perform the operations we will describe. For example, if you want to save a file, you might type the command Save in one application, press a function key labeled Save in another, or type a number corresponding to the menu choice Save in yet another. So our discussion of these operations is necessarily very general. Hopefully, with a few basic concepts in mind you will find it easier to master the applications themselves.

*E*ntering and Saving Information

Often the first thing you'll do when you start using an application is enter the relevant information. It might be text for use with a word processor, financial information for a spreadsheet, or facts and figures for a database.

Although your information is displayed on the screen, it is only in your computer's memory for as long as you are working with it. If you leave the application program, reset your computer, or turn off the power, your PC's memory will be wiped clean and you will lose all your information permanently. To avoid this, you have to store, or save, the information on your hard disk before you do any of the above things.

When you tell your PC to save some information, it does so by creating a file on the hard disk. You give the file a name before you save it so that next time you tell your PC to retrieve that information, it will know which file you are talking about. (Remember, file names must follow the rules discussed in Chapter 5.)

Most applications let you store files in directories other than the application directory or on a diskette instead of on your hard disk. You simply give the full path name when the application asks you to name the file. Although it is not necessary to store your information in a separate directory, it is a good idea. Storing information files separate from application files helps prevent accidentally writing over or deleting application files. Storing a backup version of a file on a diskette protects you against damage to your hard disk.

*R*etrieving the Information

Having saved a file, if you want to make changes or just check some information, you will have to retrieve the file from the hard disk or diskette. To do this, you give the command to read a file, and when the application asks which file, type its name. Include the full path name if the file is not in the current directory. If you forget the name of the file, use the application to list the file names in the directory where the file is stored.

*R*evising the Information

Once you have loaded the file, you can insert or delete text with your word processor, change the numbers in a spreadsheet report, or add some information to your database (not all at once, of course!).

Keep in mind that when you loaded the file, you made a *copy* and put it in your PC's memory. The original file is still safely stored on disk. The changes you make are *temporarily* in the computer's memory and don't become permanent until you save the new version of the file from memory onto disk again. There are three things you can do with the new version in your PC's memory:

- Don't save the new version at all. If you do not like the changes you have made, or if you just looked at the information but did not change it, there is no harm done. The original version is still on disk just as if you had never touched it.

- Replace the original version with the new version. If you want to overwrite the original version with the revised version, give the revised version the same name as the original version and save it on your hard disk.

- Save both versions. If you want to keep both the original version and the revised version, give the revised version a different file name if you are going to save it in the same directory, or save it on another directory.

*P*rinting the Information

To get a paper copy, or *hard copy*, of your document, you will need to print it out. Before you start printing, always make sure your printer is connected, turned on, and has paper in it. Some printers also have an on-line button that you have to press before printing. (When a printer is *on-line,* it's ready to accept printing instructions from your PC.)

Depending on the application, you will give a Print command, select Print from a menu, or press a Print function key. Then the program usually asks you to give the file name and supply some other details about how it should print the file.

Now for the work sessions. But first of all, here's a review of application programs in general.

Review

Running an application:

- Before you run an application program, you must install it on your hard disk.
- To load a program, first change the current directory to the application directory, and then type the program name.

Using an application:

- Operations are performed with commands that are typed directly, chosen from a menu, or selected using function keys.
- Entering, saving, retrieving, revising, and printing information are operations common to most applications.
- Information is saved as a file on disk. You need to supply the name of the file in order to work with it.

7

Application Work Sessions

Featuring

*Introduction to
   WordPerfect:
   entering, correcting,
   and printing text*

*Introduction to
   Lotus 1-2-3:
   worksheet basics,
   creating and printing
   a report*

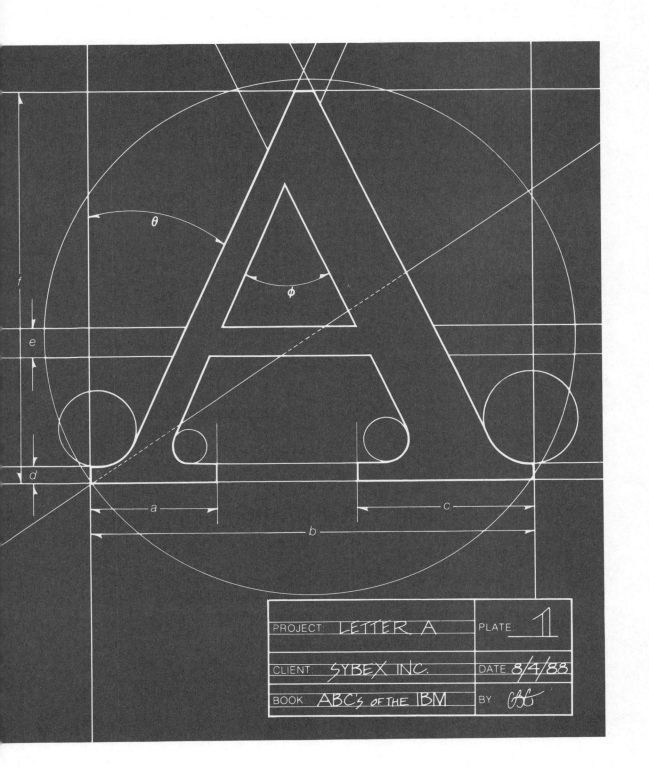

PROJECT: LETTER A   PLATE: 1

CLIENT: SYBEX INC.   DATE: 8/4/88

BOOK: ABC's of the IBM   BY: CBG

*W*ordPerfect Work Session

For some people, the main objective for buying a personal computer is to be able to do word processing. Only later do they begin to explore their PC's many other capabilities.

WordPerfect is a very powerful word-processing program and it takes a little time to master all of its commands, so we will not have time to tell you even half the story here. However, we are going to enter some text, play around with it a little, and give you enough background to get started. For more complete coverage of WordPerfect, we recommend *The ABC's of WordPerfect* by Alan Neibauer and *Mastering WordPerfect* by Susan Baake Kelly, both published by SYBEX.

If you own a word-processing program other than WordPerfect, don't skip over this work session thinking it a waste of your time. Reading through the exercises will give you an idea of how word processors work even though the commands for your program may be different.

We assume that you have already installed WordPerfect on your hard disk. Refer to the WordPerfect documentation for installation instructions.

*L*oading WordPerfect

To load the WordPerfect program:

1. Turn on your PC. DOS automatically loads from your hard disk.

2. Change the current directory to your WordPerfect directory. WordPerfect's installation instructions recommend that you name this directory wp, but you can use any name you want.

3. After the C> prompt, type

   WP ↩

   to load the WordPerfect program.

*T*he WordPerfect Screen

When you first load WordPerfect, your screen clears except for some information in the lower-right corner, and the cursor appears in the upper-left corner (see Figure 7.1). The cursor marks your typing position when you start entering text.

The screen is like a blank sheet of paper on which you can begin typing a new document. If you wanted to edit an existing document instead of starting from scratch, you could retrieve that document from your hard disk or a diskette.

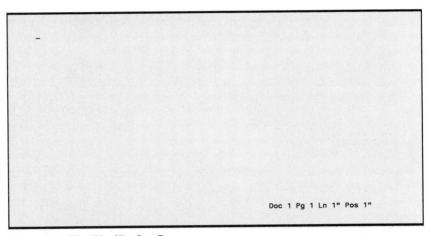

Doc 1 Pg 1 Ln 1" Pos 1"

Figure 7.1: The WordPerfect Screen

*W*ordPerfect Commands

With WordPerfect, you use your PC's function keys and several other special keys to select commands. The keys have a different meaning depending on whether you use them alone or with the ⇧ (Shift) key, Alt key, or Ctrl key. WordPerfect comes with the template shown in Figure 7.2 that fits around the function keys on your keyboard. The keyboard template acts as a menu and reminds you of the function keys' uses. If you haven't already placed this template on your keyboard, do so now.

WordPerfect®
for IBM Personal Computers

Delete to End of Ln/Pg	End/Pg Dn
Delete Word	Backspace
Go To	Home
Hard Page	Enter
◆Margin Release	Tab
Screen Up/Down	−/+ (num)
Soft Hyphen	−
Word Left/Right	←/→

© WordPerfect Corp. 1988   TMENWP01/5.0
ISBN 1-55692-200-0

Shell	Spell	Screen	Move	Ctrl	Text In/Out
Thesaurus	Replace	Reveal Codes	Block	Alt	Mark Text
Setup	◆Search	Switch	◆Indent◆	Shift	Date/Outline
Cancel	◆Search	Help	◆Indent		List Files
F1	F2	F3	F4		F5

Tab Align	Footnote	Font	Ctrl	Merge/Sort	Macro Define		
Flush Right	Math/Columns	Style	Alt	Graphics	Macro		
Center	Print	Format	Shift	Merge Codes	Retrieve		
Bold	Exit	Underline		Merge R	Save	Reveal Codes	Block
F6	F7	F8		F9	F10	F11	F12

Figure 7.2: The WordPerfect Keyboard Template

Entering Text

The first thing you will notice when you enter text is that you do not have to press ↵ at the end of a line. WordPerfect automatically wraps words around to the next line when you reach the right margin.

1. Type the paragraph below to practice entering text. Don't worry about typing mistakes at this point. If you are compelled to correct an error, press the ← (Backspace) key once to delete each wrong letter and retype correctly.

Entering text with WordPerfect is just like using a typewriter, except that it's much easier. Since words are automatically wrapped around at line endings, you don't have to worry about carriage returns until you get to the end of a paragraph.

2. Now press ↵ twice to end the paragraph and leave a blank line before typing the next paragraph:

Editing text is the best part of using a word processor. You can go back and make changes to any part of the text with instant results.

*M*oving the Cursor

When you want to make a change to existing text, you have to start by moving the cursor at the point of the change.

1. Practice using the arrow keys to move up (↑), down (↓), right (→), and left (←) through the text you just entered.

2. You can skip a whole word at a time, either forward or backward through your text. Hold down the Ctrl key and press → to move the cursor to the right one word at a time. Hold down Ctrl and press ← to move the cursor to the left one word at a time.

*I*nserting Text

One of the advantages of using a word processor is that you can insert text anywhere you want within a document.

1. To insert an extra phrase in the second paragraph, begin by moving the cursor to the *c* of the word *changes:*

   Editing text is the best part of using a word processor. You can go back and make changes to any part of the text with instant results.

2. Now type the phrase *all kinds of* (including the space after the last word).

3. Press any arrow key. That line and those that follow wrap around the right margin.

   Editing text is the best part of using a word processor. You can go back and make all kinds of changes to any part of the text with instant results.

*D*eleting Text

You can delete text one character at a time, a word at a time, or a line at a time. You can also delete whole blocks of text, but that's getting a bit fancy for this short work session. Let's delete a few characters first.

1. The ← (Backspace) key deletes one character at a time to the left of the cursor, so you must begin by moving the cursor to the right of the deletion point. Use the arrow keys to move the cursor to the space following the word *using*.

Entering text with WordPerfect is just like using_a typewriter, except that it's much easier. Since words are automatically wrapped around at line endings, you don't have to worry about carriage returns until you get to the end of a paragraph.

2. Press ← until the word *using* is deleted (that's six times including the space before the word.)

Entering text with WordPerfect is just like a typewriter, except that it's much easier. Since words are automatically wrapped around at line endings, you don't have to worry about carriage returns until you get to the end of a paragraph.

3. Now move the cursor in any direction. WordPerfect readjusts the lines in the paragraph so that they fit the margin.

Entering text with WordPerfect is just like a typewriter, except that it's much easier. Since words are automatically wrapped around at line endings, you don't have to worry about carriage returns until you get to the end of a paragraph.

You can also delete the character under the cursor. Press Del. The character that was to the right of the cursor moves underneath it.

Of course, it would have been easier to delete the word *using* all at once. Let's try this out on a word in the second paragraph.

1. Move the cursor to the *u* of the word *using*.

Editing text is the best part of using a word processor. You can go back and make all kinds of changes to any part of the text with instant results.

2. Hold down the Ctrl key and press ← (Backspace) to delete the entire word.

Editing text is the best part of a word processor. You can go back and make all kinds of changes to any part of the text with instant results.

Want to try deleting a whole line? Let's eliminate the line at the end of the first paragraph.

1. Begin by moving the cursor to the beginning of the line to be deleted.

   Entering text with WordPerfect is just like a typewriter, except that it's much easier. Since words are automatically wrapped around at line endings, you don't have to worry about carriage returns until you get to the end of a paragraph.

2. Hold down the Ctrl key and press End. WordPerfect deletes from the cursor position to the end of the line.

   Entering text with WordPerfect is just like a typewriter, except that it's much easier. Since words are automatically wrapped around at line endings, you don't have to worry about carriage

If you position the cursor within the line instead of at the beginning, WordPerfect deletes only the material from that point to the end of the line.

*T*yping Over Text

You may sometimes want to go back and type over existing text (in effect, inserting new text and deleting old text at the same time). To do this, you press the Ins key to change from Insert to Typeover mode. When you begin, WordPerfect is in Insert mode, and text that you type is inserted before the cursor. In Typeover mode, you type over text beneath and to the right of the cursor.

1. First, move the cursor to the first letter of the word you want to type over, in this case the *r* of the word *results* in the second paragraph.

   Editing text is the best part of a word processor. You can go back and make all kinds of changes to any part of the text with instant results.

2. Press the Ins key to change from Insert mode to Typeover mode. On the bottom-left corner of the screen you see the message:

   Typeover

WordPerfect expects that you'll be using Insert mode most of the time, so it displays a message only when you are in Typeover mode.

3. Type the new word *success* over the old word *results*.

Editing text is the best part of a word processor. You can go back and make all kinds of changes to any part of the text with instant success.

4. Now press Ins again to return to Insert mode.

Saving the Document

When you have entered your text and made any necessary revisions, you will want to save the document for future use.

1. Press F10. At the bottom of the screen, you see the message:

   Document to be Saved:

2. Name the file PRACTICE and save it in the root directory instead of the WordPerfect (current) directory by typing

   \PRACTICE

3. Press ⏎ to save the file. You see the message

   Saving C:\PRACTICE

Printing the Document

If you have a printer connected to your PC, you can print the document to see what it looks like on paper. Before you do this, be sure that your printer is turned on and that there is paper in it.

1. Hold down the Shift key and press F7. You see the Print menu across the bottom of the screen.

1 Full Text; 2 Page; 3 Options; 4 Printer Control; 5 Type-thru; 6 Preview: 0

When WordPerfect commands have additional options or they need more information, you see a menu. You select one of the options in the menu by typing its number. You can always type 0 to go back to whatever you were doing before you entered the command.

2. Type 1 to print the whole document.

Your printer should begin printing the document. If it doesn't, don't enter the print command again. Instead, reread your installation documentation and printer information to make sure that you installed WordPerfect correctly for your printer.

Clearing the Screen

Now that you've printed the PRACTICE document, what if you want to begin a new document? You simply clear the screen and begin typing the new document.

1. Press F7. WordPerfect asks whether you want to save the current document. The Y at the end of the prompt indicates that the default response (if you press ◀─┘) is *Yes*. You can also press Y for *Yes* or N for *No*.

    Save Document? (Y/N) Y

2. Because you already saved the document, type N for *No*. WordPerfect asks whether you want to exit the program:

    Exit WP? (Y/N) N

3. Press ◀─┘ to answer *No*. WordPerfect clears the screen.

Leaving WordPerfect

You have learned the basics of WordPerfect. As you can see, word processors are pretty easy to use. Let's leave WordPerfect and experiment with a spreadsheet program.

1. Press F7. WordPerfect asks whether you want to save the current document:

    Save Document? (Y/N) Y

2. To save the document, type Y and give WordPerfect a file name. To leave WordPerfect without saving the document, type N. WordPerfect asks whether you want to exit the program.

    Exit WP? (Y/N) N

3. Press Y to answer *Yes*. You see the DOS C> prompt.

Listing the File

If you want proof that your file is intact, list the files in the root directory by typing

DIR\ ↵

Your document should show up as

PRACTICE

unless, of course, you called it by a different name.

Lotus 1-2-3 Work Session

Of all the applications available, spreadsheets are one of the most popular, and 1-2-3 from Lotus Development Corporation is currently the best-seller in the field. Moreover, it is easy to learn! If you have a copy of Lotus 1-2-3, you can sit down at your PC with the work session that follows and go through the step-by-step instructions to create a simple report.

Although this work session is designed specifically for Lotus 1-2-3, all spreadsheets are remarkably similar. Therefore, it is worth reading through this work session even if you do not have Lotus 1-2-3 to get some idea of how a spreadsheet works. Though the commands given here are specific to 1-2-3, we have tried to make our discussion general enough to apply to any spreadsheet program.

We do not presume that in one short section we can tell you all about Lotus 1-2-3. We just want to give you the necessary steps to produce a simple report without going into all the whys and wherefores of every step. There are many others sources of information to supplement the exercise you will do here. The tutorial and reference manual that come with the program will help a lot. We also recommend *The ABC's of 1-2-3* by Chris Gilbert and Laurie Williams and *Mastering 1-2-3* by Carolyn Jorgensen, both published by SYBEX.

We assume that you have already installed 1-2-3 on your hard disk. Refer to the program documentation for installation instructions.

Loading 1-2-3

To load Lotus 1-2-3:

1. Turn on your PC. DOS automatically loads from your hard disk.

2. Change the current directory to your 1-2-3 directory. The installation instructions recommend that you name this directory 123, but you can use any name you want.

3. After the C> prompt, type

   123 ↵

   to load the program.

The 1-2-3 Worksheet

The top, left-hand portion of the worksheet is always displayed on your screen after you load the program (see Figure 7.3). The entire worksheet is too large to fit on the screen all at once, so what you see is just a small part of it. However, special commands and the cursor-movement keys let you look at any part you want.

The worksheet consists of

- **Columns**, identified by letters across the top. There are 256 columns in all, labeled A through IV. Each column is nine characters wide when you begin.

- **Rows**, identified by the numbers down the left side. There are 8,192 rows.

- **Cells**, which are the intersections of columns and rows. Cells are identified by column letter followed by row number; for example, A1.

- **The Cell Pointer**, which is a highlighted bar. The cell pointer is in cell A1 when you begin. You use the cell pointer to move around in the worksheet and enter information.

- **The Cursor**, which is a short line inside the cell pointer.

- **The Control Panel**, which is the space above the column labels. As you work, the control panel displays information, command menus, and prompts.

- **The Mode Indicator,** which is in the upper-right corner of the control panel. It reminds you what 1-2-3 is in the process of doing. When you begin, it reads **READY**, to tell you that the program is ready for you to enter information or commands.

- **The Date and Time Indicator,** which reports the current date and time. It appears in the lower-left corner when you begin. If you want, you can remove it from the display.

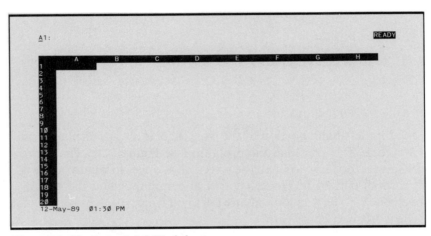

Figure 7.3: The Lotus 1-2-3 Worksheet

Creating a Report

When you create a 1-2-3 report, you can make three kinds of entries:

- **Labels** are any entries that begin with a letter—they are usually titles for the column or row; for example, Sales, Expenses, and Profit.

- **Values** are numbers; for example, 1000, 300, and 7000.

- **Formulas** perform calculations based on the values you have entered; for example, A2 − B2.

The sample report shown in Figure 7.4 will let you practice making these different kinds of entries.

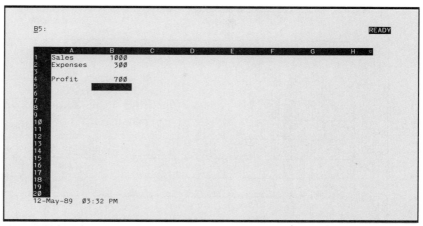

Figure 7.4: *A Sample 1-2-3 Report*

There are always three steps involved in making an entry:

1. Move the cell pointer to the cell that is to contain the entry.

2. Type the entry.

3. Press ↲ or move to another cell to enter it in the worksheet.

Figure 7.5 shows the keys you will need to create this report. The arrow keys, called Left, Right, Up, and Down, are used to move the cell pointer. The slash key (/) displays commands, and the F5 function key, called the Goto key, is used to move the cursor directly to any cell on the worksheet.

*M*oving the Cell Pointer

1. Practice using the arrow keys to move the cell pointer around in the worksheet. The → key moves the cursor to the right; the ← key moves it left; and ↑ and ↓ move it up and down.

2. Now you need to move the cursor back to cell A1 to begin creating our sample report. Press F5, and the control panel asks

   Enter address to go to:

   Notice that the control panel lists the current position of the

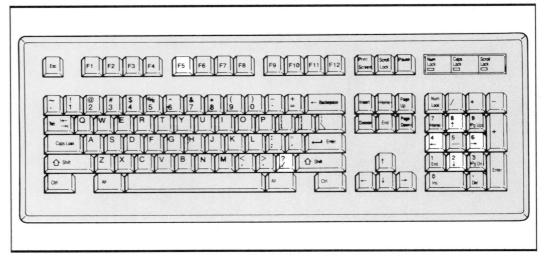

Figure 7.5: *The Slash, F5, and Arrow Keys*

cell pointer. If you do not enter another cell name, the pointer stays where it is.

3. Type A1 and press ⮐ to move the cell pointer to cell A1.

Entering Labels

1. To move the cursor to cell A2, press ↓.

2. To enter the label Sales in cell A2 and move the cell pointer down to cell A3, type

   Sales ↓

   Notice that as you type, the mode indicator changes from **READY** to **LABEL**. The mode indicator reminds you that you are now in the process of adding a label.

3. To enter the label Expenses in cell A3 and move the cell pointer down to cell A4, type

   Expenses ↓

4. To enter the label Income in cell A4, and leave the cell pointer in this cell, type

   Income ◄─┘

Entering Values (Numbers)

1. To display the **Enter address to go to**: prompt in the control panel, press F5.

2. To move the cell pointer directly to cell B2, type

   B2 ◄─┘

3. To enter the number 1000 (no comma) in cell B2 and move the cell pointer down to cell B3, type

   1000 ↓

   Notice that as you type, the mode indicator changes from **READY** to **VALUE**. It reminds you that you are in the process of entering a number (value).

4. To enter the number 300 in cell B3 and move the cell pointer down to cell B4, type

   300 ↓

Entering a Formula

1. To tell 1-2-3 you will enter a formula, type a plus sign (+).

2. To subtract Expenses (the number in B3) from Sales (the number in B2), type

   B2 – B3

   As you enter a formula, the mode indicator reads **VALUE**. The program is in the process of calculating the value that it will display in the cell.

3. To perform the calculation and enter the result, 700, in cell B4, press ◄─┘.

And now you know the basics of Lotus 1-2-3. Of course, you will be able to do a lot more when you have more experience using it, but you have already mastered creating a simple report.

The next important step is to save the report on your hard disk so that you can use it again later. First you must learn how to use 1-2-3's command menus.

*U*sing Menus

1. Press slash (/) to display the Main menu. You see

   - The **Main menu**, on the second line of the control panel.

   - The **Menu pointer**, within the Main menu. When you first display the Main menu, the Menu pointer highlights the Worksheet command.

   - A **submenu**, on the third line of the control panel. Because the Worksheet command is highlighted, the submenu displays a list of Worksheet commands.

   - MENU, as the mode indicator.

2. Press the → key. The Menu pointer moves from Worksheet to Range, and the submenu displays Range commands.

3. Press the → key again. The Menu pointer moves to Copy.

4. Type R. The Menu pointer moves back to Range. Typing the first letter of a command name is a shortcut you can use to highlight any command in the menu.

5. Press ←. Highlighting a command and pressing ← *selects* the command. When you select the Range command, the Range submenu moves to the second line of the control panel. You can now select a Range command by highlighting it and pressing ←.

6. Instead of selecting a Range command, press the Esc key. You see the Main menu.

7. Press the Esc key again. The Main menu disappears, and 1-2-3 is ready for you to enter information in the worksheet.

*S*aving *Your Report*

1. Press the slash key (/) to display the Main menu.
2. Select File. You see the File menu.
3. Select Save. 1-2-3 asks you to

   Enter save file name:

   If you already have worksheet files in the current directory, they appear on the third line of the control panel. You can select one of these files, or type the name for a new file.

4. Type

   Income

   Notice that 1-2-3 automatically uses the path name for the current directory. If you wanted to save the file in another directory, you could use the ◄— (Backspace) key to erase the current directory path name. Then type the full path name for the file. You can save the file in any directory you want.

5. Press ◄—┛ to save the file. The mode indicator changes to **WAIT** as 1-2-3 saves the file. After the file is saved, the mode indicator changes to **READY**. Your screen looks the same as it did before you displayed the Main menu.

*P*rinting *Your Report*

1. Press the slash key (/) to display the Main menu.
2. Select Print. You see the Print menu.
3. Select Printer to print your report. You see the Printer menu.

Before you can print, you must tell 1-2-3 which cells you want to print. You can print a rectangular block of one or more cells. This block is called a *range*. You identify a range with the addresses of the two most distant cells in the range separated by one or more periods. For example, A2.B4 names the range in which you have entered information. This is the range that you want to print.

4. Select Range. 1-2-3 asks you to

   Enter Print range:

   You see the name of the current cell. If you do not name another range, 1-2-3 will print the current cell.

5. Type A2.B4 and press ←⏎. You see the Printer menu again.

6. Select Go. The range you named prints.

7. Select Quit to leave the Printer menu.

Lotus 1-2-3 is now ready for you to enter new information in the worksheet.

*L*eaving 1-2-3

1. Press the slash key (/) to display the Main menu.

2. Select Quit.

3. Select Yes.

You see the DOS prompt.

*L*isting the File

After the C> prompt, type

DIR INCOME. * ←⏎

DOS lists information about the file INCOME.WK1. Notice that 1-2-3 automatically added the extension WK1 to the name that you gave the file.

*R*eview

WordPerfect:

- Is a popular word-processing program.

- Allows you to enter text and save it as a document.

- Provides automatic word wrap at line endings.
- Lets you go back and easily revise text.
- Allows you to insert, delete, and type over text; many other editing and formatting operations are possible.
- Save WordPerfect documents on disk if you want to use them later.

Lotus 1-2-3:

- Is a popular financial spreadsheet program.
- Consists of a worksheet of columns and rows that intersect to form cells for entering information.
- Allows you to make an entry by moving the cell pointer, typing the information, and entering it on the worksheet.
- Cell entries are labels, numbers, or formulas.
- Save Lotus 1-2-3 reports on disk if you want to use them later.

8

Bells and Whistles: Optional Components

Featuring

Extra disk drives

Printers

Additional memory

Color and graphics displays

Game control adapters

Plotters

Communications adapters

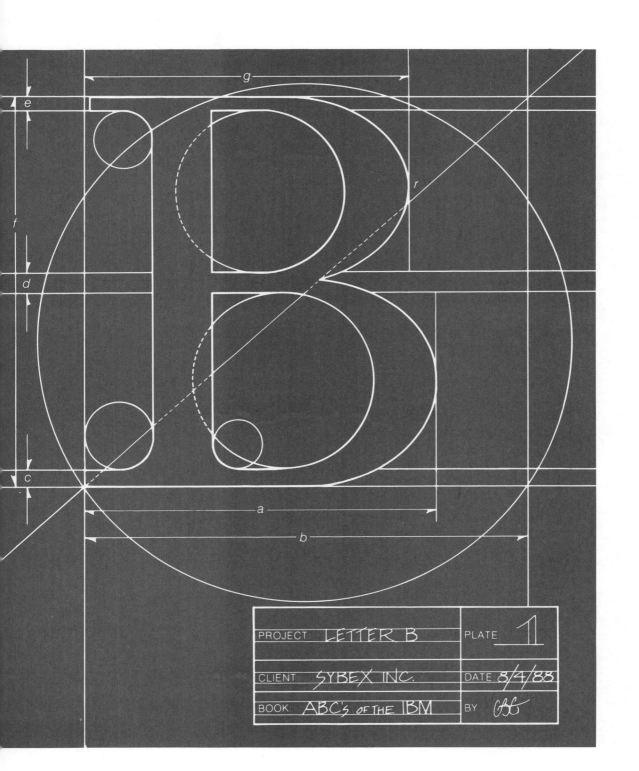

PROJECT: LETTER B   PLATE: 1

CLIENT: SYBEX INC.   DATE: 8/4/88

BOOK: ABC's of the IBM   BY: CBG

The PC is different things to different people. To some, it's a sophisticated typewriter—a word processor with a printer attached. To others, it's a fancy calculator that manages their financial affairs. Then there are those who write complex computer programs today and play video games tomorrow. The PC is a very versatile tool that can be customized for individual use by adding the application programs and bells and whistles that fit your particular needs.

Perhaps the basic PC is all you need, but you don't have to stop there! You can add printers and plotters, color and graphics, games and communications—whatever meets your needs or tickles your fancy.

Any of these additional options can be included in your initial PC purchase, or they can be added later as your needs change. The basic system unit has some empty spaces, called expansion slots, to accommodate adapters and printed-circuit boards for add-on options. The number of expansion slots is limited, so have someone check the space in your system unit before you purchase an option. Sorry—you can't have everything!

Some options are manufactured and supplied by your computer's manufacturer. Some are specially made by other companies to be compatible with the PC. Since your whole system has to work together, make sure a piece of equipment is compatible with your PC before you rush out to buy it.

This chapter gives you an overview of add-on options for the PC. If you are interested in adding options to your system, the first step is talk to your computer dealer to find out what is available. New products are constantly being developed and you will want to know what your choices are before making a purchase.

In addition, be sure you know what else is involved. Do you need special adapters or a specific amount of memory? Do you have to purchase cables and connectors separately? Take some time to check into all this ahead of time and you will be sure to end up with what you wanted.

*E*xtra Disk Drives

In this book, we have assumed you are using a system with one hard disk and one diskette drive. One diskette and one hard disk drive are almost always enough for one person, but you can add up to 26 drives (although managing so many drives is probably more trouble than it's worth). More likely, you may eventually replace your hard disk drive with one that has more storage space, or you may add a different type of diskette drive so that you can share information with others. For example, if a co-worker has a PC that uses 3.5-inch diskettes, you may want to add a 3.5-inch diskette to your system so that the two of you can easily share files.

Printers

For many people, a printer is not an option; it is an essential piece of equipment. If you will be doing word processing or producing any kind of report that needs to be on paper, you will certainly need a printer. There are three types of printers that are popular: laser printers, letter-quality printers, and dot-matrix printers.

Laser printers use technology similar to a photocopier to print one page at a time at high speed. They produce the highest quality text of the three types. With a laser printer, you can print text in a variety of sizes and styles. You can also print text and graphics on the same page. If you are using a desktop publishing program, a laser printer is essential.

Letter-quality print looks as though it comes from an IBM typewriter and is produced in much the same way, with a cartridge ribbon and a print wheel. Like a typewriter element, the print wheel can be changed to produce many different typefaces. This kind of printer is used mostly with word-processing applications or wherever high-quality letters and reports are required.

Dot-matrix print is composed of small dots that give a more uneven appearance than letter-quality print. It's fine for many jobs—program listings, memos, and drafts—but it's not good for more formal business correspondence.

The major deciding factor between the three, then, is the quality of print you require. Other considerations are speed and price. Laser printer speed is measured in pages per minute. Letter-quality and dot-matrix printer speed is measured in characters per second. Printer speed varies greatly from printer to printer. In general, laser printers are the fastest and letter-quality printers are the slowest. Dot-matrix printers are usually the least expensive. However, the decision usually comes back to the issue of print quality.

Your printer will come with a printer cable and instructions for connecting it to your PC. For some printers, you may also have to have a special adapter installed in the system unit.

*A*dditional Memory

The system unit of the PC includes a working memory which temporarily holds the program and information you are currently using. Your PC has at least 128 kilobytes of memory. Ours has 640 kilobytes. A kilobyte or K byte is around a thousand bytes, and you can think of a byte as approximately one character, so 640 K bytes of memory gives you space for about 640 thousand characters of working information. Your PC may have even more memory than ours. Greater amounts of memory are measured in megabytes. One megabyte is one thousand kilobytes.

If you work with large programs and information files you will need more memory than if you produce the odd report or memo. More memory increases the PC's ability to handle large jobs, and more is usually better. With word-processing programs, editing a large document goes faster if you have more memory since the whole document can fit in memory at one time. In addition, some application programs and other options specify the minimum amount of memory that your PC must have in order for you to run the program.

You buy your PC with as much memory as you think you will initially need. You can have more installed in the system unit later if your needs change. If you need more memory than your system unit can hold, you can purchase memory adapters to install in your PC.

*C*olor and Graphics Displays

Perhaps you want to produce illustrations, bar charts, pie charts, and graphs. Or would you like to play video games? With a color or graphics display, you can do both. Graphics and color usually go hand-in-hand; you get color on the screen as well as graphics capabilities. However, for some word processing and desktop publishing applications, you can get monochrome graphics displays that let you display different typefaces and artwork inside your written documents.

Although you use a color graphics display primarily for graphics applications, you can also use it with any other application. Usually, the quality of text on a color display is not as good as a monochrome display, so people who use their PCs mainly for word-processing prefer monochrome displays.

In addition to the color or graphics display, you will have to have a color or graphics monitor adapter installed in the system unit. Be sure that the display and the adapter are compatible.

Game Control Adapters

And since we mentioned games, you'll need a game control adapter if you want to play interactive games that use a joystick. If your computer's manufacturer doesn't offer joysticks, they can be purchased elsewhere and connected to the system unit with the game control adapter.

Plotters

A plotter is like a printer in that it gives you paper output, but there the similarity ends. A printer just prints; a plotter is an electronic artist. Instead of a print wheel, a plotter has colored pens (up to eight) that pick themselves up and move across the paper to write and draw. Plotters are used mainly with graphics applications to produce graphs and charts, as well as overhead transparencies and presentation aids.

To use a plotter with your PC, you may need to have a special adapter installed in the system unit.

Communications Adapters

Your keyboard and display allow you to communicate with your PC; a communications adapter allows your PC to communicate with other computers.

Computer communications is a wide-ranging area of technology that is constantly developing. It offers many different options. Some require the addition of an acoustic coupler or a modem (electronic, telephone-like devices), some require that your computer be connected into a communications network, and others require special software programs. What computer communications can offer you will depend entirely on your particular situation, but some possibilities are:

- Sending and receiving electronic mail messages
- Sending information across telephone lines
- Sharing information with other PC users
- Subscribing to public information services (more on these in Appendix D: Resources)
- Sharing access to a large central computer
- Using a printer or disk drive that is not even attached to your PC

A communications adapter also allows you to use other equipment such as plotters, letter-quality printers, and voice-recognition devices.

9

Checklists: If Something Goes Wrong

*F*eaturing

Troubleshooting guide
When to ask for help

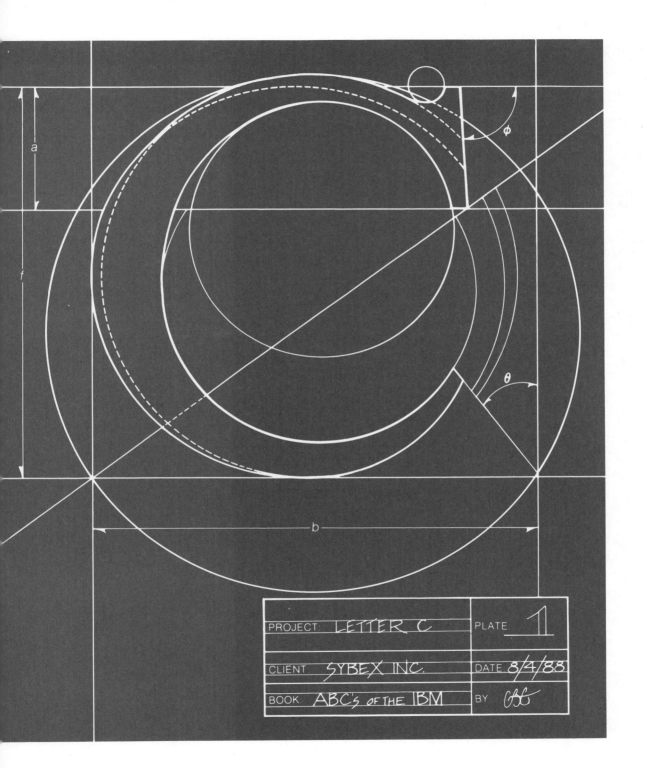

PROJECT: LETTER C   PLATE: 1

CLIENT: SYBEX INC.   DATE 8/4/88

BOOK: ABC's OF THE IBM   BY

And of course it will. Despite the high quality and reliability of the PC itself and the care you take in using it, at some point something will go wrong. When your computer won't do what you want, it can be very frustrating, so this chapter gives you some pointers for getting out of trouble.

Most problems are caused by one of two things—either you have given the computer incorrect or incomplete instructions, or something really isn't working properly. Hard as it may be to take, the first of these is usually the case. It's worth taking the time to check on yourself before you bundle up your PC and send it off for repair. Even if you are not the culprit, your service person will be able to help you much better if you can be specific about the details of the problem.

Let's start with you. Ask yourself the questions in our *You* Checklist. Does this solve the problem? Don't be embarrassed; we all make these mistakes. Just correct the problem and try again.

If the first list is no help, go on to the *PC* Checklist, which gives typical trouble areas that you can check for yourself. Although some may sound obvious (*of course* the power is on), you never know who tripped over the power cord when your back was turned.

You Checklist

— Did you get an error message? Look it up in the back of the appropriate reference manual and follow the recovery steps.

— Has DOS been installed on your hard disk? You cannot do anything until it is.

— Did you make a typing mistake? Correct the error and try again.

— Are you using the software correctly? Check the appropriate reference manual to be sure you are not confused about what you are trying to do.

— Are you looking for the file in the correct directory? Use the full path name or the DIR command to check the files in a directory.

— Are you using the correct diskette? Again, use the DIR command to list the files.

— Does the path name need a drive identifier? If the file is not on the current drive, you need to precede the path name with either A: or C:.

— Does the file name have an extension? If it does, you have to use it. Use the DIR command to check the complete file name.

— Has the diskette been formatted? You cannot store information on a new diskette until you format it using the FORMAT command.

— Are you using a defective diskette? Take the diskette out and examine it for chips, bumps, or scratches.

— Have you inserted the diskette properly? Make sure it is inside the drive as far as it will go and the drive door is closed.

— Did you close the drive door properly? Open and close it just to be sure.

— When was the last time you cleaned the diskette drives? Honestly?

— Ask someone else to take a look. We're always the last ones to notice when we've made a mistake!

*P*C Checklist

— Turn off the system power and disconnect the power cord from the wall. Always do this before you start investigating cables and connections.

— Plug another appliance into the wall outlet to see if the outlet works.

— Check that the cable connections for the keyboard and display are securely attached to the system unit. Also check the PC end of the power cord.

— Turn the contrast and brightness controls all the way to the right. If they have been turned down accidentally, you may not be able to see anything on the display. You can adjust them again later.

— Plug the power cord back into the wall and turn on the system power. The PC will run through its self test, load DOS, and ask you to enter the date and time.

— If DOS does not load properly, refer to your operations manual for more help on diagnosing the problem.

— Ask for help. Two heads are almost always better than one.

Service

If all else fails, you are going to need help from a professional service organization. Find your warranties and check your service contract. Different types of PCs come with different warranties. Most dealers also offer extended service contracts. If your PC belongs to your company, check to see if they have their own service arrangements.

Make a note of exactly how the problem occurred and any error messages you received. This is important diagnostic information.

For more information, refer to the service information in your operations manual.

A

Putting It All Together

This appendix is for those of you who have just arrived home with your brand new IBM PC/AT. It tells you everything you need to know to put your PC together. We will help you choose a good working location and unpack the shipping containers, and then go through the steps for connecting the components.

If you have a different kind of PC, you use a similar procedure. Before you assemble your PC, you may want to read through this chapter for some general guidelines, and then read the specific instructions that came with your PC.

Again, we are assuming that your computer dealer has set up your hard disk and installed DOS on it. If this is not the case, ask your dealer or your service person to do so. Although there are instructions for setting up your hard disk in your DOS reference manual, it is best to have an experienced person do it for you.

Before you begin, find a small, flat-blade screwdriver, and notice where there are grounded (3-pin) power outlets to plug your PC into when you are ready to go.

Choosing a Location

You need to take some important facts into account when deciding where to set up your PC:

1. Don't pick a place where you will be sitting with your back to a light. The glare of the light on the screen will make it difficult (sometimes impossible) to work.

2. Think about the cables and power cord. Will they be tucked out of the way or will you be inviting someone to trip over them if you put your computer here? Move the PC closer to the wall outlet if necessary.

3. Think about the back of the machine as well as the front. At some point, you will probably need to get at the rear panel. Will it be accessible without a major furniture upheaval?

4. Give the PC enough room. The system unit is quite deep and should not be balanced on the edge of a narrow desk. Most people put the keyboard in front of the system unit, so allow

space for that, too. If you prefer, you can set the keyboard to one side.

5. Give yourself enough room—more than the PC itself occupies. When you start working, you will need space for manuals, papers, diskettes, and perhaps a printer. Choose your working location with this in mind so that things will go smoothly later.

Unpacking the System Unit

1. The system unit is in the large, heavy box. Turn the container right side up, cut the binding tape, and open the box.

2. In the cardboard tray on top of the box, you will find the following items:

   - An inventory checklist for each item. Since the warranty is printed on the back of the checklists, keep these in a safe place for now and insert them in your operations manual later.

   - Power cord. Keep this handy—you'll need it soon.

   - Two manuals: *Guide to Operations* and *BASIC*. The *Guide to Operations* manual tells you all about operating your PC; the *BASIC* manual tells you how to use the BASIC programming language to program your PC.

   - A plastic bag containing some fact sheets and an IBM customer response card. Put these with the checklists for now and read and complete them later.

3. Having removed these items, take out the cardboard tray.

4. Lift out the system unit. It is tightly packed and quite heavy, so go carefully. Keep all the packing materials in case the system has to be shipped again.

5. Take the system unit out of the plastic bag and place it on a flat surface in your chosen location. You will need access to the rear and enough room to work.

6. Open the diskette drive door(s) and remove the cardboard inserts.

7. Check that the power is off. If you are facing the front of the system unit, the power switch is on the right side of the unit towards the back.

Connecting the Keyboard

1. Open the long, flat box that contains the keyboard. Take out the inventory checklist/warranty and keep it in a safe place. Put it in the operations manual later.

2. Remove the polystyrene packing material, lift out the keyboard, and take it out of its plastic bag. Keep all packing materials.

3. Place the keyboard in front of the system unit. Connect the keyboard cable to the back of the system unit (see Figure A.1). Make sure you push the cable connector on firmly.

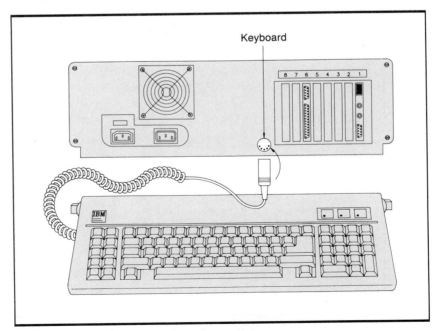

Figure A.1: Connecting the Keyboard

Connecting the Display

1. Turn the display container right side up, cut the binding tape, and open the container.

2. Take out the inventory checklist/warranty and keep it in a safe place. Put it in the operations manual later.

3. Remove the display. Like the system unit, it is tightly packed, so you will have to struggle a bit. Take off the packing materials and plastic bag and store them with the others.

4. Put the display on top of the system unit.

5. Take the plastic bag off the cables on the back of the display.

6. Connect the display cables to the back of the system unit (see Figure A.2). Push both cable connectors on firmly, then tighten the retaining screws on the right-hand connector.

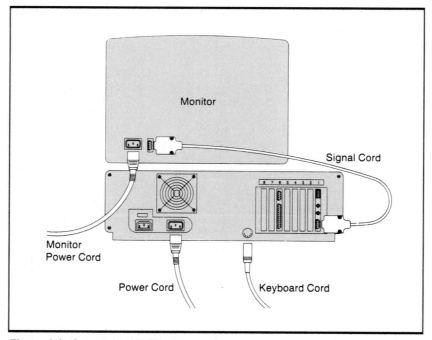

Figure A.2: Connecting the Display

Connecting the Power Cord

1. Connect one end of the power cord to the back of the system unit (see Figure A.3).

2. Plug the other end of the power cord into a grounded wall outlet.

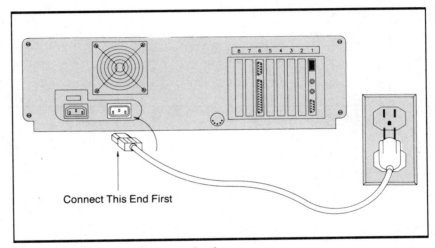

Connect This End First

Figure A.3: Connecting the Power Cord

Adjusting the Keyboard

The keyboard is designed to be level or to tilt and is adjusted with the knobs on the top corners. Squeeze the knobs in and turn them toward you to tilt the keyboard, away from you to make it level (see Figure A.4). Try it both ways so that you can decide which feels best for you.

That's it! Take a minute to make sure your PC is set up in a good location, then go back to Chapter 1 to find out what all these components do, or to Chapter 2 where we tell you how to turn on the power and start using your PC.

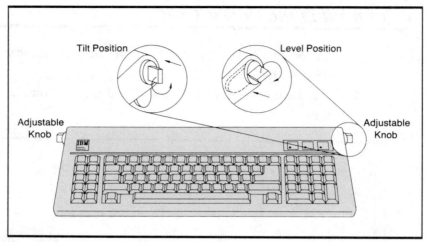

Figure A.4: *Adjusting the Keyboard*

APPENDIX

B

Using a PC without a Hard Disk

If your PC does not have a hard disk, your diskettes become more important. Your PC does not even know how to start DOS without a copy of DOS on a diskette, and you must use program diskettes to run applications. Because you rely so much on diskettes, making backup copies of them is very important.

In this appendix we discuss how to use your PC without a hard disk. We assume that you have two diskette drives. The one on top is drive A: and the one on the bottom is drive B:. (If your diskette drives are side-by-side, the one on the left is drive A: and the one on the right is drive B:.)

*T*urning on Your PC

When you turn on your PC, it does not load DOS automatically.

1. Turn the contrast and brightness knobs on the front of the display fully to the right. These may be located on the side or back of your monitor. Once your PC is warmed up, you can adjust the knobs, but if you don't start with them fully on, you might not see anything on the screen.

2. Turn on the power with the switch on the right side of the system unit (or, the power switch may be on the back).

When you first turn on your PC, it runs through a quick test to make sure everything is in working order. If the test is successful, three things happen:

1. After the system warms up (this takes a few moments), a blinking underscore called the *cursor* appears at the top left of the screen.

2. You hear a short beep.

3. A message like the following one appears at the top of the screen:

The IBM Personal Computer DOS Version 3.30
© Copyright International Business Machines Corp. 1981, 1987
© Microsoft Corp. 1981, 1986

Or, you may be prompted to enter a bootable diskette and press any key.

Your PC is turned on and ready use, but it can't do anything for you until you load DOS from your diskette.

L oading DOS

If you have a PC without a hard disk, you can load DOS in one of two ways: by inserting the DOS diskette and turning on the power, or, if the power is already on, by inserting the diskette and resetting the PC. When you reset, you clear the information currently stored in memory and read in new information from another diskette. The information you load remains in the PC's memory until you either reset the computer again or turn off the power.

Assuming your PC is still turned on, follow these steps to load DOS:

1. Insert the DOS diskette in drive A: (the top or left-hand drive).

2. Close the drive door.

3. Reset your PC by holding down the Ctrl and Alt keys on the left of the keyboard, and pressing the Del key on the right.

4. The cursor blinks at the top of the screen, the red drive light goes on, and you hear some whirrs and clicks that tell you that DOS is being loaded into your computer.

5. Then you see the current-date message. For example,

   Current date is Tue 1-01-1980
   Enter new date:_

C opying a Diskette

Use the DISKCOPY command to make backup copies of your diskettes. Practice by making a copy of your DOS diskette.

1. Insert the DOS operating diskette in drive A:. (Load DOS from the startup diskette if you have not already done so.)

2. Insert a blank diskette in drive B:.

3. To copy the DOS diskette in drive A: onto the blank diskette in drive B:, type

   DISKCOPY A: B: ↵

4. Your PC displays the message:

   Insert source diskette in drive A:
   Insert target diskette in drive B:
   Strike any key when ready

   Since you have already inserted the diskettes, press any key to begin the copy operation.

5. The red lights on the diskette drives go on and you hear a whirring sound and the message **Copying 1 side(s)** is displayed. When the diskette has been copied, you are asked

   Copy another (Y/N)?

6. You do not want to copy another diskette so type N (for no).

7. Remove the DOS diskette from drive A:, return it to its protective sleeve, and store it in a safe place. From now on, use the backup copy as your everyday, working copy of DOS.

8. Remove the backup copy of DOS from drive B:. Before you put it away, take time to label and write-protect it.

*L*oading an Application

There are two steps to loading any application:

1. Insert DOS into drive A: and load it as usual. Loading DOS is almost always the first thing you do when you want to use your PC. Application programs will not work unless DOS is there first.

2. Remove the DOS diskette and insert the application program diskette, or backup copy, in drive A:. Then type the program

name (usually an abbreviation) and press ⏎ to load the program.

As you use the program, keep the program diskette in drive A:. Save your work files on another diskette in drive B:.

Self-Loading Applications

Many applications allow you to combine loading DOS and loading the application program into one step by copying the relevant parts of DOS and the application program onto a new diskette. The application then becomes self-loading. The application reference manual will tell you if the application can be made self-loading. If it can, follow these steps:

1. Insert DOS into drive A: and load it as usual.

2. Remove but save the foil write-protect tab from the application program diskette (or the backup copy, if you have one), and insert the diskette in drive B:.

3. At the DOS prompt, type

   SYS B: ⏎

   This command copies the operating system files from the DOS diskette to the diskette in drive B:.

4. When the DOS prompt appears again, type

   COPY A:COMMAND.COM B: ⏎

   This copies the DOS command files to the diskette in drive B:.

5. When the copy operation is complete, remove the application diskette from drive B: and replace its write-protect tab.

The application diskette is now self-loading—you can load both DOS and the application program by putting the application diskette in drive A: and turning on the power, or by resetting your computer (press Ctrl, Alt, and Del). Remember, you must type the name of the application at the DOS prompt to start the application.

APPENDIX

Glossary: or, A Little Bit of Computerese for the Converted

Backup

A backup is a duplicate copy of a file or diskette. When you make such a copy, you are *doing a backup*. Back up a hard disk using the DOS BACKUP command; back up a diskette using the DOS DISK-COPY command; back up a file using the DOS COPY command. You can also purchase special backup programs for use with your hard disk.

Bit

Short for Binary DigIT. That tells you a lot, doesn't it! Well, we could go on about binary digits being 0 and 1 and computers operating on ON/OFF signals where ON is 1, and OFF is 0, but, honestly, would you be any the wiser? You might want to remember that there are eight bits in a byte, but then again, you might not.

Boot

When you load the operating system, DOS, you are *booting* your computer. Loading DOS by turning the power on is a *hard boot;* resetting is a *soft boot*.

Bug

Anything that makes the computer or its software stop working as planned. The story goes that an insect trapped inside an early computer caused it to malfunction; little did that insect know it was headed for immortality!

Byte

The unit of measurement for computer storage and memory. A byte can store about one character of information. Bits and bytes go together; there are eight bits in a byte.

Chip

Also called a silicon chip. This tiny sliver of silicon, containing incredibly complex circuits, is the heart and soul of your computer and the single technological advance that shrank it to desktop size.

CPU

Short for central processing unit. It is the place in the system unit of your PC where all information is processed. Also known as a microprocessor.

Crash

A complete malfunction of your computer, much worse than a bug. Originally meant that the read/write head inside the diskette drive had crashed into the disk, but has now become a generic term for any major breakdown.

CRT

Short for cathode ray tube. The tube itself is a television tube that allows information to be shown on the display screen, but the term is used to refer to computer terminals and displays that use CRTs.

Daisy Wheel

The kind of print wheel used in many letter-quality printers. It has a central hub and lots of spokes with printable characters on the ends. Looks *something* like a daisy.

Data

Hardly a computer term any more. Everyone gathers and processes data these days. Really just means information.

Database

A collection of files that are grouped together because they have something in common. They can be sorted and accessed selectively and thus form valuable sources of information. When you receive junk mail, chances are your name has been pulled out of a large computer database.

Debug

Correcting a hardware or software error—getting the bugs out—is debugging. Sometimes debugging is done by people; sometimes it is done by special software programs.

Default

Something the computer assumes unless you tell it otherwise. For example, the PC automatically uses the default drive, C:, unless you tell it you want to use drive A:.

Downtime

If your system crashes, it will be out of action, or *down*, for a while. If the crash occurred at 1:45 pm and the system is not repaired until 4:03 pm the same day, downtime was 2 hours and 18 minutes.

Floppy Disk

Another name for a diskette. Sometimes just called a *floppy*.

Flowchart

A sort of road map to a computer program. Programmers design a flowchart to help them write a program. It tells them what should follow what and where to go if a particular event occurs.

Hard Copy

A printed paper copy of anything your computer produces, from a computer program listing to a word-processing document.

Head

A small magnetic device inside a disk drive that reads and writes information on disks.

Input

Anything you put into your computer—commands, programs, instructions. Your input tells the computer what to do.

Interactive

When you give your computer an instruction and it responds, you are interacting with each other. Most application programs are interactive.

Interface

A piece of hardware or software that allows communication between your computer and another device. For example, a printer interface lets you transfer information from your PC to a printer.

Kilobyte

Approximately one thousand bytes (1,024 to be precise), usually abbreviated Kb or K bytes.

Kludge

Everybody has their own definition of this term. For us, it's hardware or software that has been put together sloppily in great haste. It's recognizable by wires sticking out and maybe a little smoke. It works, but nobody is sure why. Your PC is *not* a kludge.

Laser Printer

A high-speed printer that prints one full page of high-quality text and/or graphics at a time. Used with desktop publishing and other applications where printer quality is important. Often shared by several PC users.

Line Feed

To advance by one line. Most printers have a line feed button that you press to move the paper up by one line.

Line Printer

A high-speed printer capable of printing an entire line at a time. Used with large, shared computers rather than individual personal computers.

Logged Drive

Another way of saying the current or default disk drive.

Megabyte

A million bytes, usually abbreviated Mb or M bytes.

Memory

The part of the computer that stores programs and information needed to perform the current operation. There are different kinds of memory (see RAM and ROM).

Microcomputer

A complete, small, computer system, like your PC.

Microprocessor

See CPU.

Mouse

A small, rectangular device that sits to the side of your keyboard. Some programs use the mouse to control a pointer on the display. You move the pointer by moving the mouse on your desk. You press one of the mouse's buttons to select objects or commands.

Nerd

A cross between a human being and a computer. Usually pale and thin with red eyes and a vocabulary consisting only of the terms in this glossary. Also sometimes called a techno-junkie. This is for your edification only—*never* call someone a nerd.

Network

A group of interconnected computers that can communicate and share, send, and receive information among themselves.

Operating Environment

A program that changes the way you interact with your PC. Instead of requiring you to type DOS commands to communicate with your PC, most operating environments let you select commands with a mouse and view files through windows on your display.

Output

What your computer comes up with after acting on your input. The output may be displayed on the screen, stored on a disk, or printed, depending on your instructions.

Peripheral

Any additional equipment you attach to your computer. Printers and disk drives are typical peripherals.

RAM

Random Access Memory—the part of the computer's memory that temporarily holds your program and instructions while you are working with them. When you turn the computer off, RAM loses its memory, and your information along with it, unless you have stored the information on disk.

Read a Disk

To copy information from a disk into the computer's memory. You can't use the information stored on a disk until it has been read into memory.

Response Time

The interval between you telling the computer to do something and it acting on your instructions. The shorter the better.

ROM

Read Only Memory—the part of the computer's memory that holds information permanently. With your PC, BASIC is in ROM and is stored there at all times, even when you turn the PC off and go home for the day.

Utility

Software used for regularly performed operating system operations such as managing or recovering files. Several steps are combined to carry out a complete operation with only one instruction from you. Makes your life easier, and the computer work for its living.

Window

An area on your screen that displays the contents of a file. Normally, you can move and change the size of a window. Some application programs let you work with two files at once by displaying them in different windows. Operating environments use windows to let you work with files from more than one application.

Write to a Disk

To copy information from the computer's memory onto a disk. Keeps a permanent copy on disk for future use—the computer's memory is only temporary.

D

Resources

*M*agazines

There are dozens of magazines that can help you to learn more about your PC. Here we list several general purpose magazines. You may be able to get samples from your computer dealer or at your local bookstore. In addition, software manufacturers often send newsletters to registered application users. These newsletters might give you tips for using the program more efficiently, profile other users, or describe new products. Other good sources of information are the professional societies to which you belong. They can refer you to magazines for your particular profession. For example, there are magazines aimed at personal computer users in the fields of medicine, law, and agriculture.

Business Software, M & T Publishing
Monthly, $25/year
Send subscription inquiries to: Business Software Magazine, P.O. Box 3713, Escondido, CA 92924.

For managers who use PCs. Includes articles on databases, financial applications, and business graphics. Provides product reviews, examples of computer use, and tips.

BYTE, McGraw-Hill Inc.
Monthly, $22 year
Send subscription inquiries to: BYTE Subscriptions, P.O. Box 7643, Teaneck NJ 07666. Phone (800) 423-8272; in NJ (800) 367-0218; outside US (201) 837-1318.

For the experienced computer user. Articles and information are technical in nature and are intended for people who want to know how their computer is put together and what makes it work.

Computer Shopper, Computer Shopper of Titusville, Inc.
Monthly, $21/year
Send subscription inquiries to: Computer Shopper, Inc., 5211 S. Washington Ave., P.O. Box F, Titusville, FL 32781. Phone (305) 269-3211.

For all microcomputer users. Software and hardware reviews, new product information, book reviews, bulletin board and user group information.

80 Micro, IDG Communications/Peterborough Inc.
Monthly, $24.97/year
Send subscription inquiries to: 80 Micro, Subscription Department, P.O. Box 981, Farmingdale, NY 11737.

For users of Tandy MS-DOS PCs. Includes general news, product reviews, and how-to articles.

Family and Home Office Computing, Scholastic, Inc.
Monthly, $19.97/year
Send subscription inquiries to: Family and Home Office Computing, P.O. Box 51334, Boulder CO 80321-1334. Phone (303) 447-9330.

For people who use their computers at home. Includes ideas for using computers in a home office, hardware and software reviews, features on computers for education and entertainment, and tutorials.

InfoWorld, InfoWorld Publications, Inc.
Weekly; Free of charge to qualified buyers of microcomputers and related products. To all others, $100/year.
Send subscription inquiries to: InfoWorld, P.O. Box 5994, Pasadena, CA 91107. Phone (818) 577-7233.

For all microcomputer users. Software reviews, new product information, book reviews, computer literacy for the novice, industry reports.

Online Access, Online Access Publishing Group, Inc.
Bimonthly, $24.95/year
Send subscription inquiries to: Subscription Services, Online Access, 5616 W. Cermak Road, Cicero, IL 60650. Phone (800) 922-9232 or in Illinois (312) 922-9292 collect.

For business users on information services. Includes news, reviews, and guides to services.

PAQ Review, Redgate Communications
Bimonthly, $15/year
Send subscription inquiries to: Redgate Communications, 660 Beachland Boulevard, Vero Beach, FL 32963.

For users of COMPAQ PCs. Includes news, reviews, and tips.

PC Clones, Patch Communications, Inc.
Monthly, $21/year
Send subscription inquiries to: PC Clones Magazine, 511 Washington Avenue, Titusville, FLA 32780. Phone (800) 327-9926; in Florida (305) 269-3211.

Focuses on PCs manufactured by companies other than IBM. Includes hardware and software reviews, general information, and articles on increasing productivity.

PC Magazine, Ziff-Davis Publishing Company
Biweekly, $39.97/year
Send subscription inquiries to: PC Magazine, P.O. Box 54093, Boulder CO, 80322. Phone (303) 447-9330.

For a general audience. Includes hardware and software information, software reviews, and general news.

PC Resource, IDG Communications/Peterborough Inc.
Monthly, $24.97/year
Send subscription inquiries to: IDG Communications/ Peterborough Inc., 80 Elm Street, Peterborough, NH 03458. Phone (603) 924-9471.

For a general audience. Includes software and hardware reviews, how-to articles, and program listings.

PC Tech Journal, Ziff-Davis Publishing Company
Monthly, $39.97/year
Send subscription inquiries to: PC Tech Journal, P.O. Box 2886, Boulder CO, 80322-2886. Phone (800) 525-0643 or (303) 447-9330.

For the experienced computer user. Includes technical articles and information on topics such as data communications, application development, and data management.

> *PC WEEK,* Ziff-Davis Publishing Company
> Weekly, $160/year
> Send subscription inquiries to: Customer Service Department, PC WEEK, P.O. Box 5970, Cherry Hill, NJ 08034. Phone (609) 428-5000.

For business users of microcomputers. Includes product information, reviews, and business news.

> *PC World,* PCW Communications, Inc.
> Monthly, $29.90/year
> Send subscription inquiries to: PC World Subscription, Subscriber Services, P.O. Box 55029, Boulder, CO 80322-5029. Phone: (800) 642-9606.

For a general audience. Includes hardware and software information, software reviews, personality profiles, user-group and bulletin board updates.

> *Personal Computing,* Hayden Publishing Company, Inc.
> Monthly, $18/year
> Send subscription inquiries to: Personal Computing, P.O. Box 51788, Boulder, CO 80321. Phone (800) 525-0643.

For a general audience. Includes new product information, hardware and software reviews, application information, and interviews.

> *Personal Publishing,* Hitchcock Publishing Company
> Monthly, $24/year
> Send subscription inquiries to: Hitchcock Publishing Company, 25W550 Geneva Road, Wheaton, IL 60188. Phone (312) 665-1000.

For users of desktop publishing programs. Includes tips and reviews.

Publish!, PCW Communications Inc.
Monthly, $39.90/year
Send subscription inquiries to: Subscriber Services, P.O. Box 55400, Boulder, CO 80322. Phone (800) 222-2990 or (402) 895-7284 in Nebraska.

For users of desktop publishing programs. Includes news, hardware and software reviews, tips, and page makeovers.

Information Services

The widespread use of computers, especially personal computers, has created an information explosion. More facts and figures are available now than ever before. Information can give you an advantage in business, in school, in planning your career, and in making purchase decisions for your home. With a small investment in a communications adapter (see Chapter 8) and the software to use it, your PC can plug you into the information you need. We discuss three types of information services in this section: public information services, database vendors, and electronic mail services. Because these services are continuously evolving, contact the vendors listed for current information.

Public Information Services

Public information services offer subscribers the latest news and information from a variety of sources. By subscribing to the service of your choice, you can turn your PC into an electronic newspaper, mail box, travel agent, and more. Public information services give you access to special interest group information, software, bulletin boards, electronic mail, online games, and the services of several database vendors (described in the next section).

CompuServe

CompuServe Information Service, Inc.
500 Arlington Centre Blvd.
Columbus, OH 43220
(800) 848-8990 or (614) 457-8650 in Ohio and outside the contiguous U.S.

Delphi

General Videotext Corporation
Blackstone Street
Cambridge, MA 02139
(800) 544-4005 or (617) 491-3393 in Massachusetts

GEnie

General Electric Information Services
401 N. Washington Street
Rockville, MD 20850
(800) 638-9636

The Source

1616 Anderson Road
McLean, VA 22102
(800) 336-3330 or (703) 821-8888 in Virginia and outside the contiguous U.S.

Database Vendors

Database vendors give you access to information. Usually the database is compiled by another firm, although database vendors sometimes compile their own databases. Some databases are available exclusively from one vendor, while others are available from virtually all vendors. Membership fees and rate schedules vary among vendors and their different products. Send for more information from several database vendors before you sign up with one. Some databases are also available from the public information services described in the previous section.

BRS/SEARCH
BRS/COLLEAGUE
BRS/After Dark
BRS Information Technologies
1200 Route 7
Latham, NY 12110
(800) 468-0908 or (518) 783-7251, collect

BRS services give you access to over 100 databases. BRS/SEARCH is the main system, and is designed primarily for librarians and other information professionals.

Data-Star
> 485 Devon Park Drive, Suite 110
> Wayne, PA 19087
> (800) 221-7754 or (215) 687-6777 in Pennsylvania

Data-Star provides European business information through over ninety databases. Subjects include business news, medicine, chemistry, engineering, and the environment.

DIALOG
DIALOG Business Connection (DBC)
The Knowledge Index (KI)
DIALOG Information Service, Inc.
> 3460 Hillview Avenue
> Palo Alto, CA 94304
> (800) 334-2564

DIALOG gives you access to over 250 databases. DIALOG Business connection offers the most business-oriented DIALOG databases in a menu-driven format. The Knowledge Index offers about 40 DIALOG databases at reduced rates after normal business hours.

Dow Jones News/Retrieval Service
> P.O. Box 300
> Princeton NJ, 08543-0300
> (609) 452-1511

Offers about 35 databases. Over half are produced by Dow Jones. Focuses on financial information, up-to-the-minute stock and commodity quotes. You can trade stocks on the system. Gateway to MCI Mail. They contain stock quotes, news, and the full text of the *Wall Street Journal*.

NewsNet
NewsNet, Inc.
945 Haverford Road
Bryn Mawr, PA 19010
(800) 345-1301 or (215) 527-8030 in Pennsylvania
Gives you access to the full text of more than 300 trade, industry, and investment newsletters, wire services, and TRW business profiles and credit reports.

NEXIS
Mead Data Central
9393 Springboro Pike
P.O. Box 933
Dayton, OH 45401
(800) 227-4908
Contains complete text of hundreds of magazines, newspapers, wire services, and industry newsletters.

Pergamon ORBIT Infoline, Inc.
8000 Westpark Drive
McLean, VA 22101
(800) 421-7229

Offers bibliographic citations and abstracts in over 70 individual databases. Focuses on technical information.

VU/TEXT
VU/TEXT Information Services, Inc.
325 Chestnut Street
Philadelphia, PA 19106
(800) 258-8080 or (215) 574-4400 in Pennsylvania

Offers the full text of about 25 metropolitan newspapers, stock quotes, and some bibliographic databases.

Western Union InfoMaster
1 Lake Street
Upper Saddle River, NJ 07458
(800) 247-1373, department 509 or (201) 825-5000

Gives you access to databases from several vendors including BRS, DIALOG, NewsNet, Orbit, and VU/TEXT.

Wilsonline
H. W. Wilson Company
    950 University Avenue
    Bronx, NY 10452
    (800) 622-4002 or (800) 538-3888 in New York

Offers on-line versions of the printed works, such as the *Reader's Guide to Periodic Literature*, published by the H.W. Wilson Company.

Electronic Mail Services

Electronic mail services let you send messages to other PC users across the country and even, with some services, around the world. When you subscribe to an electronic mail service, you receive an electronic mailbox on a central computer. Other users of the electronic mail system can send messages to your mailbox, and you can send messages to them. You check for mail regularly, for example once a day, and can copy messages you want to keep from your mailbox to your PC.

AT&T Mail
AT&T Customer Assistance Center
    P.O. Box 3505
    New Brunswick, NJ 08903
    (800) 367-7225 ext 720
    (800) 624-5672

EasyLink
Western Union Telegraph
    1 Lake Street
    Upper Saddle River, NJ 07458
    (800) 527-5184

MCI Mail
MCI Communication Corporation

1150 10th St. NW, Suite 800
Washington, D.C. 20036
(800) 444-6245 or (202) 293-4255

Index

Selections from The SYBEX Library

DOS

The ABC's of DOS 4
Alan R. Miller
275pp. Ref. 583-2
This step-by-step introduction to using DOS 4 is written especially for beginners. Filled with simple examples, *The ABC's of DOS 4* covers the basics of hardware, software, disks, the system editor EDLIN, DOS commands, and more.

ABC's of MS-DOS
(Second Edition)
Alan R. Miller
233pp. Ref. 493-3
This handy guide to MS-DOS is all many PC users need to manage their computer files, organize floppy and hard disks, use EDLIN, and keep their computers organized. Additional information is given about utilities like Sidekick, and there is a DOS command and program summary. The second edition is fully updated for Version 3.3.

Mastering DOS
(Second Edition)
Judd Robbins
722pp. Ref. 555-7
"The most useful DOS book." This seven-part, in-depth tutorial addresses the needs of users at all levels. Topics range from running applications, to managing files and directories, configuring the system, batch file programming, and techniques for system developers. Through Version 4.

Understanding DOS 3.3
Judd Robbins
678pp. Ref. 648-0
This best selling, in-depth tutorial addresses the needs of users at all levels

with many examples and hands-on exercises. Robbins discusses the fundamentals of DOS, then covers manipulating files and directories, using the DOS editor, printing, communicating, and finishes with a full section on batch files.

MS-DOS Handbook
(Third Edition)
Richard Allen King
362pp. Ref. 492-5
This classic has been fully expanded and revised to include the latest features of MS-DOS Version 3.3. Two reference books in one, this title has separate sections for programmer and user. Multi-DOS partitons, 3 1/2-inch disk format, batch file call and return feature, and comprehensive coverage of MS-DOS commands are included. Through Version 3.3.

MS-DOS Power User's Guide,
Volume I
(Second Edition)
Jonathan Kamin
482pp. Ref. 473-9
A fully revised, expanded edition of our best-selling guide to high-performance DOS techniques and utilities—with details on Version 3.3. Configuration, I/O, directory structures, hard disks, RAM disks, batch file programming, the ANSI.SYS device driver, more. Through Version 3.3.

DOS User's Desktop Companion
SYBEX Ready Reference Series
Judd Robbins
969 pp. Ref. 505-0
This comprehensive reference covers DOS commands, batch files, memory enhancements, printing, communications and more information on optimizing each user's DOS environment. Written with step-by-step instructions and plenty of examples, this volume covers all versions through 3.3.

MS-DOS Advanced Programming
Michael J. Young
490pp. Ref. 578-6
Practical techniques for maximizing performance in MS-DOS software by making best use of system resources. Topics include functions, interrupts, devices, multitasking, memory residency and more, with examples in C and assembler. Through Version 3.3.

Essential PC-DOS (Second Edition)
Myril Clement Shaw
Susan Soltis Shaw
332pp. Ref. 413-5
An authoritative guide to PC-DOS, including version 3.2. Designed to make experts out of beginners, it explores everything from disk management to batch file programming. Includes an 85-page command summary. Through Version 3.2.

The IBM PC-DOS Handbook (Third Edition)
Richard Allen King
359pp. Ref. 512-3
A guide to the inner workings of PC-DOS 3.2, for intermediate to advanced users and programmers of the IBM PC series. Topics include disk, screen and port control, batch files, networks, compatibility, and more. Through Version 3.3.

DOS Instant Reference SYBEX Prompter Series
Greg Harvey/Kay Yarborough Nelson
220pp. Ref. 477-1, 4 ¾" × 8"
A complete fingertip reference for fast, easy on-line help:command summaries, syntax, usage and error messages. Organized by function—system commands, file commands, disk management, directories, batch files, I/O, networking, programming, and more. Through Version 3.3.

Hard Disk Instant Reference SYBEX Prompter Series
Judd Robbins
256pp. Ref. 587-5, 4 ¾" × 8"
Compact yet comprehensive, this pocket-sized reference presents the essential information on DOS commands used in managing directories and files, and in optimizing disk configuration. Includes a survey of third-party utility capabilities. Through DOS 4.0.

Understanding Hard Disk Management on the PC
Jonathan Kamin
500pp. Ref. 561-1
This title is a key productivity tool for all hard disk users who want efficient, error-free file management and organization. Includes details on the best ways to conserve hard disk space when using several memory-guzzling programs. Through DOS 4.

WORD PROCESSING

Visual Guide to WordPerfect
Jeff Woodward
457pp. Ref. 591-3
This is a visual hands-on guide which is ideal for brand new users as the book shows each activity keystroke-by-keystroke. Clear illustrations of computer screen menus are included at every stage. Covers basic editing, formatting lines, paragraphs, and pages, using the block feature, footnotes, search and replace, and more. Through Version 5.

The ABC's of WordPerfect 5
Alan R. Neibauer
283pp. Ref. 504-2
This introduction explains the basics of desktop publishing with WordPerfect 5: editing, layout, formatting, printing, sorting, merging, and more. Readers are shown how to use WordPerfect 5's new features to produce great-looking reports.

The ABC's of WordPerfect
Alan R. Neibauer
239pp. Ref. 425-9
This basic introduction to WordPefect consists of short, step-by-step lessons—for new users who want to get going fast. Topics range from simple editing and formatting, to merging, sorting, macros, and more. Includes version 4.2

Mastering WordPerfect 5
Susan Baake Kelly
709pp. Ref. 500-X

The revised and expanded version of this definitive guide is now on WordPerfect 5 and covers wordprocessing and basic desktop publishing. As more than 200,000 readers of the original edition can attest, no tutorial approaches it for clarity and depth of treatment. Sorting, line drawing, and laser printing included.

Mastering WordPerfect
Susan Baake Kelly
435pp. Ref. 332-5

Step-by-step training from startup to mastery, featuring practical uses (form letters, newsletters and more), plus advanced topics such as document security and macro creation, sorting and columnar math. Through Version 4.2.

Advanced Techniques in WordPerfect 5
Kay Yarborough Nelson
586pp. Ref. 511-5

Now updated for Version 5, this invaluable guide to the advanced features of WordPerfect provides step-by-step instructions and practical examples covering those specialized techniques which have most perplexed users—indexing, outlining, foreign-language typing, mathematical functions, and more.

WordPerfect 5 Desktop Companion
SYBEX Ready Reference Series
Greg Harvey/Kay Yarborough Nelson
1006pp. Ref. 522-0

Desktop publishing features have been added to this compact encyclopedia. This title offers more detailed, cross-referenced entries on every software features including page formatting and layout, laser printing and word processing macros. New users of WordPerfect, and those new to Version 5 and desktop publishing will find this easy to use for on-the-job help.

WordPerfect Tips and Tricks (Third Edition)
Alan R. Neibauer
650pp. Ref. 520-4

This new edition is a real timesaver. For on-the-job guidance and creative new uses, this title covers all versions of WordPerfect up to and including 5.0—covers streamlining documents, automating with macros, new print enhancements, and more.

WordPerfect 5 Instant Reference
SYBEX Prompter Series
Greg Harvey/Kay Yarborough Nelson
316pp. Ref. 535-2, 4 ¾" × 8"

This pocket-sized reference has all the program commands for the powerful WordPerfect 5 organized alphabetically for quick access. Each command entry has the exact key sequence, any reveal codes, a list of available options, and option-by-option discussions.

WordPerfect Instant Reference
SYBEX Prompter Series
Greg Harvey/Kay Yarborough Nelson
254pp. Ref. 476-3, 4 ¾" × 8"

When you don't have time to go digging through the manuals, this fingertip guide offers clear, concise answers: command summaries, correct usage, and exact keystroke sequences for on-the-job tasks. Convenient organization reflects the structure of WordPerfect. Through Version 4.2.

WordPerfect 5 Macro Handbook
Kay Yarborough Nelson
488pp. Ref. 483-6

Readers can create macros customtailored to their own needs with this excellent tutorial and reference. Nelson's expertise guides the WordPerfect 5 user through nested and chained macros, macro libraries, specialized macros, and much more.

The ABC's of Microsoft Word (Third Edition)
Alan R. Neibauer
461pp. Ref. 604-9

This is for the novice WORD user who

wants to begin producing documents in the shortest time possible. Each chapter has short, easy-to-follow lessons for both keyboard and mouse, including all the basic editing, formatting and printing functions. Version 5.0.

Mastering Microsoft Word on the IBM PC (Fourth Edition)
Matthew Holtz
680pp. Ref.597-2

This comprehensive, step-by-step guide details all the new desktop publishing developments in this versatile word processor, including details on editing, formatting, printing, and laser printing. Holtz uses sample business documents to demonstrate the use of different fonts, graphics, and complex documents. Includes Fast Track speed notes. For Versions 4 and 5.

Advanced Techniques in Microsoft Word (Second Edition)
Alan R. Neibauer
462pp. Ref. 615-4

This highly acclaimed guide to WORD is an excellent tutorial for intermediate to advanced users. Topics include word processing fundamentals, desktop publishing with graphics, data management, and working in a multiuser environment. For Versions 4 and 5.

Mastering DisplayWrite 4
Michael E. McCarthy
447pp. Ref. 510-7

Total training, reference and support for users at all levels—in plain, non-technical language. Novices will be up and running in an hour's time; everyone will gain complete word-processing and document-management skills.

Mastering MultiMate Advantage II
Charles Ackerman
407pp. Ref. 482-8

This comprehensive tutorial covers all the capabilities of MultiMate, and highlights the differences between MultiMate Advantage II and previous versions—in pathway support, sorting, math, DOS

access, using dBASE III, and more. With many practical examples, and a chapter on the On-File database.

The Complete Guide to MultiMate
Carol Holcomb Dreger
208pp. Ref. 229-9

This step-by-step tutorial is also an excellent reference guide to MultiMate features and uses. Topics include search/replace, library and merge functions, repagination, document defaults and more.

Advanced Techniques in MultiMate
Chris Gilbert
275pp. Ref. 412-7

A textbook on efficient use of MultiMate for business applications, in a series of self-contained lessons on such topics as multiple columns, high-speed merging, mailing-list printing and Key Procedures.

Introduction to WordStar
Arthur Naiman
208pp. Ref. 134-9

This all time bestseller is an engaging first-time introduction to word processing as well as a complete guide to using WordStar—from basic editing to blocks, global searches, formatting, dot commands, SpellStar and MailMerge. Through Version 3.3.

Practical WordStar Uses
Julie Anne Arca
303pp. Ref. 107-1

A hands-on guide to WordStar and MailMerge applications, with solutions to comon problems and "recipes" for day-to-day tasks. Formatting, merge-printing and much more; plus a quick-reference command chart and notes on CP/M and PC-DOS. For Version 3.3.

Mastering WordStar Release 5
Greg Harvey/David J. Clark
450pp. Ref. 491-7

This book is the ultimate reference book for the newest version of WordStar. Readers may use Mastering to look up any word processing function, including the new Version 5 and 5.5 features and enhancements, and find detailed instructions for fundamental to advanced operations.

WordStar Instant Reference
SYBEX Prompter Series
David J. Clark
314pp. Ref. 543-3, 4 ¾" × 8"

This quick reference provides reminders on the use of the editing, formatting, mailmerge, and document processing commands available through WordStar 4 and 5. Operations are organized alphabetically for easy access. The text includes a survey of the menu system and instructions for installing and customizing WordStar.

Understanding WordStar 2000
David Kolodney/Thomas Blackadar
275pp. Ref. 554-9

This engaging, fast-paced series of tutorials covers everything from moving the cursor to print enhancements, format files, key glossaries, windows and MailMerge. With practical examples, and notes for former WordStar users.

SPREADSHEETS AND INTEGRATED SOFTWARE

Visual Guide to Lotus 1-2-3
Jeff Woodward
250pp. Ref. 641-3

Readers match what they see on the screen with the book's screen-by-screen action sequences. For new Lotus users, topics include computer fundamentals, opening and editing a worksheet, using graphs, macros, and printing typeset-quality reports. For Release 2.2.

The ABC's of 1-2-3 Release 2.2
Chris Gilbert/Laurie Williams
340pp. Ref. 623-5

New Lotus 1-2-3 users delight in this book's step-by-step approach to building trouble-free spreadsheets, displaying graphs, and efficiently building databases. The authors cover the ins and outs of the latest version including easier calculations, file linking, and better graphic presentation.

The ABC's of 1-2-3 Release 3
Judd Robbins
290pp. Ref. 519-0

The ideal book for beginners who are new to Lotus or new to Release 3. This step-by-step approach to the 1-2-3 spreadsheet software gets the reader up and running with spreadsheet, database, graphics, and macro functions.

The ABC's of 1-2-3
(Second Edition)
Chris Gilbert/Laurie Williams
245pp. Ref. 355-4

Online Today recommends it as "an easy and comfortable way to get started with the program." An essential tutorial for novices, it will remain on your desk as a valuable source of ongoing reference and support. For Release 2.

The Complete Lotus 1-2-3
Release 2.2 Handbook
Greg Harvey
750pp. Ref. 625-1

This comprehensive handbook discusses every 1-2-3 operating with clear instructions and practical tips. This volume especially emphasizes the new improved graphics, high-speed recalculation techniques, and spreadsheet linking available with Release 2.2.

The Complete Lotus 1-2-3
Release 3 Handbook
Greg Harvey
700pp. Ref. 600-6

Everything you ever wanted to know about 1-2-3 is in this definitive handbook. As a Release 3 guide, it features the design and use of 3D worksheets, and improved graphics, along with using Lotus under DOS or OS/2. Problems, exercises, and helpful insights are included.

Lotus 1-2-3 Desktop Companion
SYBEX Ready Reference Series
Greg Harvey
976pp. Ref. 501-8

A full-time consultant, right on your desk. Hundreds of self-contained entries cover every 1-2-3 feature, organized by topic, indexed and cross-referenced, and supplemented by tips, macros and working examples. For Release 2.

Advanced Techniques
in Lotus 1-2-3
Peter Antoniak/E. Michael Lunsford
367pp. Ref. 556-5

This guide for experienced users focuses on advanced functions, and techniques for designing menu-driven applications using macros and the Release 2 command language. Interfacing techniques and add-on products are also considered.

Lotus 1-2-3 Tips and Tricks
Gene Weisskopf
396pp. Ref. 454-2

A rare collection of timesavers and tricks for longtime Lotus users. Topics include macros, range names, spreadsheet design, hardware considerations, DOS operations, efficient data analysis, printing, data interchange, applications development, and more.

Mastering Symphony
(Fourth Edition)
Douglas Cobb
857pp. Ref. 494-1

Thoroughly revised to cover all aspects of the major upgrade of Symphony Version 2, this Fourth Edition of Doug Cobb's classic is still "the Symphony bible" to this complex but even more powerful package. All the new features are discussed and placed in context with prior versions so that both new and previous users will benefit from Cobb's insights.

The ABC's of Quattro
Alan Simpson/Douglas J. Wolf
286pp. Ref. 560-3

Especially for users new to spreadsheets, this is an introduction to the basic concepts and a guide to instant productivity through editing and using spreadsheet formulas and functions. Includes how to print out graphs and data for presentation. For Quattro 1.1.

Mastering Quattro
Alan Simpson
576pp. Ref. 514-X

This tutorial covers not only all of Quattro's classic spreadsheet features, but also its added capabilities including extended graphing, modifiable menus, and the macro debugging environment. Simpson brings out how to use all of Quattro's new-generation-spreadsheet capabilities.

Mastering Framework III
Douglas Hergert/Jonathan Kamin
613pp. Ref. 513-1

Thorough, hands-on treatment of the latest Framework release. An outstanding introduction to integrated software applications, with examples for outlining, spreadsheets, word processing, databases, and more; plus an introduction to FRED programming.

The ABC's of Excel
on the IBM PC
Douglas Hergert
326pp. Ref. 567-0

This book is a brisk and friendly introduction to the most important features of Microsoft Excel for PC's. This beginner's book discusses worksheets, charts, database operations, and macros, all with hands-on examples. Written for all versions through Version 2.

Mastering 1-2-3 Release 3
Carolyn Jorgensen
682pp. Ref. 517-4

For new Release 3 and experienced Release 2 users, "Mastering" starts with a basic spreadsheet, then introduces spreadsheet and database commands, functions, and macros, and then tells how to analyze 3D spreadsheets and make high-impact reports and graphs. Lotus add-ons are discussed and Fast Tracks are included.